THE JOURNAL OF A MAN

VOLUME I

A witness of faith, discernment, and perseverance

SECOND EDITION

ADAM JAROSZ

ABOUT THE AUTHOR

Adam Jarosz is a husband, father of four, and a man forged in the wild mix of faith, family, and adventure. With over twenty years of experience in youth ministry, entrepreneurship, and leadership, Adam brings heart and grit to the journey of becoming who we're called to be.

Iron Ore: The Journal of a Man is more than a book—it's a raw and honest chronicle of a young man being shaped in the fire of real life. Through journal entries and reflections rooted in Catholic tradition, Adam invites readers into a path of purpose, challenge, and authentic masculinity.

As the founder of Righteous Co., Adam is on mission to awaken the soul of men—to equip them for life's battle, call them into brotherhood, and form them into the men God made them to be. When he's not writing or leading retreats, he's coaching others to step into the adventure of life fully alive.

COVER IMAGE *Unsplash*
COVER DESIGN & BOOK LAYOUT *Jeremy Dolph*
AUTHOR PHOTOGRAPH *Dan Ottaviano*
EDITED *Emma Fair*

© 2024 by Adam Jarosz
All rights reserved

Printed in the United States of America

To Marisol Jarosz, our first
August 9, 2016
Rest in Peace, Baby

Volume I

2008 – 2016

(23 – 31 years old)

Contents

Preface
13

Raw Ore
24

Refiners Fire
35

The Hammer
62

The Whetstone
86

The Sword
103

Epilogue
134

The devil tempts that he may ruin. God tests that He may crown.

ST. AMBROSE

Preface

Men will ask two questions about life, "Where am I going?" and "How do I get there?" These are questions that haunted me through my twenty's. Without guidance and purpose, these two questions can drive a man to destruction. The sad part is, for the 21st century man there is so much to distract and pull us away from a life of fulfillment—lies of doubt, materialism, sex, and power among others.

This is my witness on how I started to learn the answer to these questions for my life. By sharing my personal journal, I am passing on to you what I have learned along the way. My goal is to shed light on the inner prayer, discernment, joy, and pain of one man and servant of the Lord finding his purpose.

As I sit here writing this years after the first entry was put to paper, I see how far I've come in formation. It was a difficult but conscience decision to have my first published book be an open book on my interior life. This is a raw work from the primordial scratches at pursuing a better masculinity than where I was. Everything from rudimentary writing to vulnerability of weakness—the following journal entries have taken place over the course of an eight-year period. During this time I have developed from a raw piece of iron ore into an instrument, something likening a sword, a capable weapon. All of this because I know I was called. I give credit to my Blacksmith, Our Father, for hammering me into shape by putting experiences and people into my life to break and make me. I've learned that every hammer strike is one more strike to shape me into the man I have been called to be. The final design is unknown to all but the eye of the Blacksmith and only revealed by time. You too are called.

Along with the journal entries, I have posed reflections and challenges for you to contemplate and take action to. From my perspective of writing this experience, I don't feel polished or done. Actually, I will continue this theme with volumes as I grow. As of my last edits to this book, I finished the fourth volume of the journal coming off the Adirondack mountains. The hope of much more life is in front of me to refine. The idea of Righteous Co. was formed in the coals of this fire and it is a work well underway to independence.

My dream is to help inspire you to take action—to start raw and share your story. Your life, as is mine, is a witness to those around you. Understand that you come from great Love and for hard things. The witness of God's work in your life needs to be told too. Pick up the pen and get started with your own journal. Don't be afraid. Discipleship is shared and our Blacksmith had done great things for us, even in the hardest of moments.

The many entries into the journal have taken place on the go: in sand, up against trees in the woods, chapels, between ministry sessions, and in various places I called home. Oftentimes my thoughts are quickly jotted down, a snapshot moment of emotion; others are more carefully construed. My voice in this is my personal prayer and conversation with the Lord. I will guide the reader along the virtually unedited posts with a narrative that serves three points: faith, discernment, and perseverance.

Because apparently it takes me a long time to get something through my head, there are swaths of time that I find myself wrestling with decisions to be made. Actions to be taken. It took a long time to learn and own this process. It's a theme that I find again and again. It's simple really—discern, decide, and act. But it took so long to get it. And even longer to find the courage to do so.

I am witness of what it means to grow in this. These are important lessons for all of us. I offer this up from a position of vulnerability as I fail constantly here. If you struggle with spinning your wheels over and over again, it's ok. I've been there. Don't fret it. Stay diligent and just remember to never give up. Do the deep work and play the long game. And remember to, never give up.

This book is written with three audiences in mind, first of which is my family tree. I came to this idea much later as I thought of "who would ever read something like this". And my greatest hope for that answer is that my children, grandchildren, and great-grandchildren will read this if no one else. I started this when I was twenty-three years old. I was years away from finding my wife and certainly had no view of what, or if for that matter, my family would happen to look like. My kids will never know me as that young man. They'll never know my hopes and dreams, fears and struggles. What it cost to rise to a great call. I want them to know that our family humbly came from great love and through hard things. If I ever get called home to Heaven early, I want them to *know* me. That this father, this forefather for the next generations, stood for listening to our God and that they too play a role in their space and time to that same end. This is a love letter to them. To you, my wife, my daughters, my sons—I love you.

Secondarily, this is for men. To realize you are iron that should be placed in the care of a Great Blacksmith to form you. Raw ore is filled with impurities that unless refined, stays weak and unpliable. It takes high heat and physical hammering to remove those things. Ironworking requires intention, action, and labor. The theme of this book and the subsequent opportunities from it come from this process. You'll see how the heating and repetitious hammering in my own life made me stronger. I was formed from weakness for great purpose with my Vocation of marriage. It took a long time to even be ready to find my wife—and that was only the beginning.

For the men out there, who struggle to find their purpose and fire, don't discount the role of faith. If you struggle to believe or are bored with it, you haven't dug into the depths. Get hungry. When you hand over the helm of your ship, God will use you in ways you could not have imagined. It's an adventure of virtue and development that only a heavenly general can strategize for you. You become a weapon of good, a well-conditioned soldier for the fights and traps that lay ahead. Your life gains purpose and rhythm. It takes endurance and perseverance, patience and strength, effort and rest. It all starts with a commitment to prayer and God will hone your skills and make you the best man you can be. It doesn't matter where you start, you just have to begin, again if need be, and keep at it.

By no means does this mean that women can't take this advice also, but speaking as a man, this is crafted with the masculine heart on full display. I know that men need to rise to the occasion. Masculinity has been trampled by society and as a man among a growing tide of others rejecting that forced position for something greater. This is a rally cry for you, man—no matter your season of life or much success you've seen or how much failure you've endured. You are good enough, and you are made with immense purpose in this world for the next. Don't be fearful, don't be anxious, don't be complacent.

Lastly, this goes out to the faithful. As a disciple who has served and labored for the Church at various levels for over two decades, I have been through unique situations that have presented themselves as lessons to me. I hope others can relate to them or draw from them as well. If you are a servant in the Church, you might share in some of these experiences. If you belong to a Church community, know that those that serve you: clergy, minister, staff, or volunteer—walk a hard journey and need your support. When they are supported, they can support others. They too have a unique story. Ask them to share it with you. Understand the struggles they face; they are often underfunded, under-appreciated, over worked, and may serve in a toxic environment. This is compounded by a growing secular society increasingly hostile to those who stand the ground on faith. Moreover, these individuals may be experiencing the personal struggles of doubt, self-esteem, self-harm, debt, and relationship troubles that seem to manifest in ministry circles.

Love them, go all in for them; contribute time, talent, and treasure. *Build a relationship.* These are the working arms and legs so the rest can be the hands and feet of God. While not perfect, they need your help to realize the best they can offer. Break down the walls and barriers that exist by moving first. Break the ice and start new by building the relationship. Sometimes that starts by offering a cup of coffee and listening to what they hope for.

I've seen too many of my peers in ministry hurt in ways they shouldn't be in a Christian environment. This goes out to them, especially those in youth ministry. After working in a variety of jobs in my life from doing construction, kitchens, working in a factory, selling—the hardest job I've known mentally, spiritually, and emotionally has been ministry.

I write this as a devout Catholic. For the friends, family, peers, and strangers and from whatever background you may come from—know this. Christ is King. The Holy Spirit is lighting souls on fire. And they want us to get to the Father. I have dedicated this book and my labor of Righteous Co. to the Holy Spirit, come what may. You will see my prayer language through that lens. No matter your denomination, join me in the fellowship we have in our Triune God, for They are the ultimate Dreamer and Doer.

Do you want to know who you are? Don't ask. Act! Action will delineate and define you.

THOMAS JEFFERSON

Prologue

We begin my journey with my role as a volunteer Core Member for my home parish in 2008; I was a young man at the age of 23. Ambitiously driven on a career path and prowling for opportunities, I always made sure I was making time to serve my church. I started the journal as a volunteer Core Member joining our youth for the first time at summer camp. As a gift for being a part of the experience, everyone received a journal to catalog the experience. I wasn't into journaling; never had been.

At this time, tensions in my life's direction were eating at me; I was faced with many serious questions: What's my purpose? Where am I going? Who's going to be my wife? I *really* don't want to be a priest.

The priesthood haunted me. By this time, it was already knocking down the door on my heart and I was resisting hard. I loved the idea of marriage. Having a wife and family seemed like the easy choice but I was, what I humbly thought, the perfect candidate for the priesthood; single, young, energetic, dashingly handsome, charismatic, and passionate for the faith. Of course, I'd make a great priest right? At this point I felt that I was doomed for it, like a *marked* man. This was not an overnight sensation but a battle drawn out over years. As I was getting closer to the Lord, I felt that I was getting closer to being a priest. The tension was strong inside of my prayer. I would run down to the beach often by myself and throw stones at the sunset, "What do You want me to do?!" I would wager that I would do anything God asked as long as it wasn't the priesthood, then the call would rise up stronger.

At the same time I was always on the lookout for the future Mrs. Jarosz, dating on and off. I thought I knew what I was looking for but nothing was sticking. Quietly a romantic at heart, I had hopes that I would get there. At 17, I made a commitment to a girlfriend that I'd save sex for marriage, for my wife. Imperfectly, the commitment lasted but the relationship didn't. I was now fighting for my wife. On the front burner was the thought that I had better be saving this for my spouse and not the priesthood. I don't think I would have gotten far if the goal was the other way around.

So with this soup boiling inside of me and the right encouragement from the camp speakers placed by the Holy Spirit, I was inspired to write. I began to put my prayers down. This new ground proved to be awkward and unnatural. I kept pushing forward, line by line. After going back to read my early entries, I was rather embarrassed by them. My handwriting is awful, especially since I was writing in a small book often in my lap or on a tree. My writing style felt like a five-year-old's. But hey, that's where I began, so that's our starting point.

As time went on, I kept returning to the journal as lessons or experiences developed. I found value in writing them down as a source of prayer and self-reflection. I improved my handwriting by relearning cursive. Then, I reached deeper as I became serious about keeping my written prayer. I found that it helped me track my journey and see how God was moving in my life. That rawness refined over time and created the theme that named the book. I saw myself being crafted for something greater than I had vision for. I was being formed as a man. Although it was never my original intent, I eventually felt prompted to share the journey that has led me to where I am today. It became apparent that the lessons I learned were not just for me.

I'd like to encourage you to pick up your pen and start seeing how God is forming you. Be a witness to it. Catalog what God is teaching you. When you look back you can see His footsteps alongside you every step of the way. Capture the big movements of life and see how you too are formed from Iron and with great purpose.

With that, let's begin.

God allows us to experience the low points in life in order to teach us lessons that we could learn in no other way.

C.S. LEWIS

CHAPTER ONE

Raw Ore

A long time ago a young apprentice approached his master, who was busy in the workshop, and said, "Master, how do you find the purest ore to work with?"

The master grabbed a clump from his pile and staring into the dark, dirty piece that looked like so many others and replied, "Purity isn't found, it's *refined* by fire and hammer."

◆

My early journal was as raw as can be. When iron is pulled from the ground it is rough and dirty. It's an element that is abundant in the universe and like today's world, there is plenty of raw souls waiting to be refined. When you think about where you stand today, how would you define yourself in the process of formation? Are you straight from the Earth? Have you experienced heat and hammer? Are you well polished and ready for anything?

July 6, 2008

Our Father, who art in Heaven. Hallowed be thy name. Thy Kingdom come. Thy Will be done, on Earth as it is in Heaven. Give us this day our daily bread, and forgive us our trespasses, as we forgive those who trespass against us and lead us not into temptation but deliver us from evil.

—Amen.

Lord, thank you for allowing me this experience. Thank you for growing me and letting me experience you in a real way. Thank you for answering my prayer on vocations and I continue that prayer for patience, honor, and dignity.

Keep moving forward! "I have Your plan."

July 7, 2008
Message to my wife.

I love you babe. I think about you often, I wonder who you'll be or what your name is. I've spent my life praying for you.

More recently, I have wondered whether or not God would bless me with you. I thought He was calling me into the priesthood. It has caused me a lot of heartache and distress. I wanted to do the Lord's will and of course still do, but I wanted to be married to you. The Lord resolved my worry with some comedy. One night, I was praying about my discernment and I was... reading the bible. I don't read that often enough by the way. Anyways... He pulled up all of these verses for me to read, one that really sticks out to me went something like this, "If a man needs a wife, then get him a wife." I forget where that was from or what the other ones I read said but they affirmed it. (Later recalled, it was actually Tobit 8:6: "It is not good for man to be alone...").

But that was the Lord saying, "She's out there and you will marry her."

I have and continue to save sex for you. It is the hardest thing I have ever done but I do it for you. <u>Only</u> with God's help <u>is it possible.</u>

I bet you're beautiful inside and out and I wanted to write this to you with God. He put us together. He made us, He made our personalities and I thank Him everyday for you. By His good graces and by His love are we together. I owe Him my life and my everything. Help me to honor Him by building our family, relationship, and our love around Him.

I am twenty three right now and I don't know you yet, but I love you, more than words can describe. I'm trying to show patience in finding you but it's difficult. I'm sure when I'm finally patient, the Lord will introduce us. Until then, I wait and look.

Yours truly,
Adam
(You can kiss me now)

July 8, 2008

How do I think God will pour out His grace on me in reconciliation?

OK Lord, this paper and pen are not cooperating with me. Funny. (Ink was running out on the paper, looks awful.)

I really don't know how Your Grace is going to pour out on me. Reconciliation is a weak spot in my faith. I go sparingly but when I do go I feel Your absolution.

Lord, I feel tired and drained after seeing Your live passion today. I felt sorrow and emotion. I wanted to cry. Thank you for letting me feel that inside even if I try to suppress it from the outside.

Thank you for dying for us, for me.

Thank you for showing patience with me and for helping me over and over again with the same sins, including lust.

Thank you for loving me, and giving me the heart to love others.

July 10 2008

Fears Given Up

Oh Holy Spirit, I am fearful and that is not from You. I give this list up to You to take and destroy. I don't want these fears. They not only hold me back from You but they hold me back in life. I am afraid of...

- Spiders

- Heights
- Flying
- Evil
- Dying
- Our country's collapse
- Your will for me being a priest
- Random fears/unnamed fears

I raise these up to You, not so I can just pawn them off but so You and I both know of the work that lies ahead to defeat them. I continue to seek understanding of You. Amen.

2 Timothy 1:7: "See God in everything."

July 10 2008

Adoration was weird today. Matt's talk led me to write my fears. I was supposed to lift those fears during Adoration; however I prayed for something else instead.

I didn't want to pray for myself so I lifted up our nation. I prayed for protection from corruption and decay. I prayed for our institutions and our freedom, for the fall of evil and corrosive socialism, the rise of good in our culture, government, economy, military, and religion. For our actions overseas and our soldiers so they may be just and righteous.

When I wrote down my fears I tried to draw a dove of the Holy Spirit, but it turned out to look like an eagle. I didn't plan it but the Holy Spirit knew where my heart was.

LORD I ACCEPT YOUR <u>WILL</u>!

LORD I TRUST IN <u>YOU</u>!

July 31, 2008

OK so here's a fantastic "God story" that is incredible and almost indescribable…

So I've been seeing this girl, Carlie, and have been on a few dates that have been great. I've never had a relationship grow like this. Lord, Your fingerprints are all over this and I love it.

Last Friday was the Ice Cream Social and that whole day was awesome. Since then I feel like I have dropped the ball with her. Actually, that night I meant to tell her how I felt about her but I couldn't get it together. It's been eating at me ever since. It's Thursday now and my heart has just been burning with angst to tell her. I felt like today was do or die, she leaves for vacation on Saturday and if I didn't tell her how I felt I could lose her. At least that's how I felt.

I called her earlier but no answer. So I left a message. I just needed to talk to her mono-e-mono. I had this elaborate plan (joke about a bench being a time machine "Hey if you could go back in time… I would go back to Friday and tell you how I felt" or something.) Yeah. Anyways...

All day I was really hoping that she would call back. My emotions were ridiculous. I felt like a teenaged schoolgirl. I couldn't call again, that would be creepy.

Notes, text messages, smoke signals were just stupid and wouldn't cut it. So I waited and prayed.

It was about sunset and I went to the mall to check out a sale... this sounds like a chick diary... I really was feeling compelled to leave the house and get some fresh air. So I went to the mall. After I got there I realized that I didn't want to be there and left after five minutes. My heart was aching bad and I was frantically asking God for help with this. I was just saying, "God have her call me".

At this point I was losing hope and thought I'd run over to the beach, watch the sunset, and pour out my heart to God. I was feeling like crap on a log.

I get to Woodlawn Beach and the sun had already sunk behind the horizon. Light was dimming fast and I had this urge to park and get to the sand quickly before I missed too much of it. The sky was still orange. I had time.

I get through the woods via the walkway and hit the sand. I was praying, "Lord if I can't get a hold of her, will You send a message from my heart to hers and have her call me?"

I'm on the sand walking and a few people are left watching the sunset, others are packing up to leave. I walk towards the water and notice two girls walking away from the lifeguard stand. I didn't think anything of it, my mind was preoccupied and the light was getting low. As I got closer I started thinking, "Could that be her?" No way...

Yes it was. Carlie was with a friend. I was blown away. Did God set this up? I had my chance to tell her but I didn't want to in front of her friend. After some awkward small talk, we parted. I started for the shore and they started back to the car. I still needed to tell her but I locked up. After a moment, I knew I couldn't let her get away without telling her what I needed to say. I couldn't blow the opportunity.

I ran back to them, to her. "Hey wait! I need to steal her for five minutes."

So I got the five minutes I was looking for and I laid it out for her. We have potential and who knows, we may be reading this later. (Sorry if you're not her.)

God has a plan and today was awesome. After we left, my heart was cured from the grief and angst that plagued it. God knew the pain I was in no matter how insignificant it is to the world and brought the two of us together even if was just to close it up.

I don't know what will happen between the two of us but I do know God is with us. He is walking with me and He will not lead me astray.

I thank You Lord. I praise You Lord. Thank you for your help today.

◆

That is where I started, with those few entries to capture the awkward moment of my life when I started to write down my prayer. It was just a snapshot of raw ore, ready for more. The camp experience was powerful for the teens and for the ministry after that trip. I found in that trip, a voice that would gain steam. A voice that would develop along with my faith and be a witness to God's work in me as I developed into the man I will become. Long before this, I gave my life over to the Lord and trusted where He would take me, whether I would like it or not.

I started to see how God was working in my life on a continual basis; it was like riding a train and not a series of one-offs like genie wishes. Instead of, "I pray I get or don't get," it was "all aboard to destination unknown." My involvement with our youth ministry as a Core Member helped me keep my feet in the fire. Weekly youth group, seasonal retreats, and marquis trips such as World Youth Day in Germany, a pilgrimage to Italy, and trainings in Arizona all helped heat my ore.

I figured my destination was around the corner, when in fact it would be a much longer journey than I ever bargained for. Little did I know, that the Refiner's Fire would be so hot and it was that heat that would begin to soften me to be pliable. When you become receptive to what's going on in life, you start to see God's hand in everything. I was blessed to start seeing the Invisible Hand through difficult times.

Questions:

1. Where are you at right now in your life? How is it going?

2. Are you who you want to be? Why or why not?

3. How is your faith life? Is prayer a daily routine?

Challenges:

— Start a journal to track your prayer and God's work in your life. Get a new, sturdy journal. Keep at it and pick it up again when you stop. Let God use you and refine you. Track it.

— Build up your prayer life. Either start or push a little bit more. Spend 10 more minutes a day talking to God than you are now. Write that time in your calendar right now and set an alarm.

*It is easier to build
strong children
than
to repair
broken men.*

FREDERICK DOUGLAS

CHAPTER TWO

Refiners Fire

The apprentice was having a hard time with his fire. He piled his coal up high but couldn't get it to stay hot. Embarrassed by his difficulty with this seemingly easy task, he sheepishly approached the master, "Master, I can't get my fire to stay hot enough to work with. What am I missing?"

The master knew all along what he needed but had waited for him to ask. "You'll need to make use of the tools at your disposal. Oxygen is the key. Give it air and fan the flames as needed." The master then pointed to the dusty blower on the floor and the apprentice went to work fanning his flame.

◆

Heat as a part of the smelting process creates change in an element like iron. The process is used to extract impurities from the metal. Impurities in metallurgy weaken the object. Blacksmith's will need to generate great heat for the melting point of iron, at least a balmy 2,500°. How has God allowed for great heat in your life? What impurities have risen in you?

June 2, 2010

It's been almost two years since I last wrote in my prayer journal. In some ways some things never change; in other ways, they do.

As I progress, I'm still seeing what God has in store for me. I used to worry about what I'm being called for. If I'm doing the right plan. More recently, I've been realizing that I am doing God's will. The whole struggle is forging me into the man I am supposed to be.

I've been reading <u>Wild at Heart</u> by John Eldridge, an awesome book about being a warrior in life. Everything he was talking about was already peddling through my head before I got started, but this made it alive and gave it direction. Here is a quote that hit me hard because I felt like it was being spoken to me,

> *"Be strong and courageous, because you will lead these people to inherit the land I swore to them. Be strong and very courageous. Have I not commanded you? Be strong and courageous. Do not be terrified; do not be discouraged, for the Lord your God will be with you wherever you go."*
> Josh 1:6-7, 9

Last weekend, I was working with the film company and traveled down to Voorhees, New Jersey. This trip challenged my spiritual and emotional mettle.

I went to the store before work on Saturday morning to grab some food and the newspaper to read for the long day. As I walked to the line to cash out, a strange but familiar feeling came over me. I couldn't place it at the time but it felt like a migraine was coming on. The dizziness and pre-aura feeling in the head were tell-tale but something new happened. I lost power to my legs. Standing in the aisle with my groceries, I had to do a "controlled crash" and land on my hands. I pulled it off as if I had to tie my shoes because I didn't want to make a scene. No one noticed the episode. After a moment, I was able to stand again proceed through checkout. At this point a terror started in me. I was freaked out. I have never had anything like that happen to me. I've had bad migraines before and my first cluster migraine sent me to the hospital and crushed me with scary temporary disabilities, but never had I lost the use of my legs.

As the day went on, I feared about the possibilities of what it was. The migraine feeling was growing. It feels like a weakness. Your whole body goes weak and your head gets cloudy before one happens. I started recognizing the need to get medicine for it. Excedrin is usually my go to for these. If I take it at the right time, it stops it in its tracks. If I don't, hold on to your butts.

So after returning to the store and picking up the miracle med, I could feel it working. The growing sensations dissipated. What a relief. Disaster averted. The last thing I wanted to do was have a migraine... in New Jersey.

My mind still raced around the episode with my legs however. My spiritual war had begun. My thoughts led me to different terrible outcomes from cancer, to epilepsy, Lou Gehrig's, aneurysm, multiple sclerosis, really anything that popped into my head but all my thoughts ultimately came to this, "What if I die?" Note to self, don't Google symptoms.

I thought about how fragile my life was. How serious this could be. Losing control over your legs is a pretty big deal. How should I prepare mentally if I was dying? Very strange, because I love my life. I wasn't checking out early because I wanted to. It scared me and for the first time ever, I was far from home when something bad happened and far away from anyone who would back me up.

To my relief, the Excedrin smacked the migraine from starting up fully and I continued working until the next day when I left. However the monster sat in my head waiting.

After a long day working I was finished and prepared to head home around sundown. I had to be back in the studio the next morning to get our orders done. I was only on the job a short time at this point so I didn't want to screw up. Time was of the essence.

Stopping at the store to gas up, I picked up some salty jerky, energy drinks, and sugary milks. Yum. The combination of sodium, caffeine, exhaustion, a stumped migraine, and focused driving ahead led to a perfect storm for the "big one."

Somewhere around Syracuse, I got the feeling again and recognized it. I started getting auras and became very sensitive to the light. The reflectors and headlights from the passing cars attacked my eyes. On top of that, I was driving through a rainstorm in a narrow construction zone. The headache didn't start yet but I knew I was in trouble.

When I get migraines, usually once or twice a month, it's not just a tormenting headache; it's usually joined with light and touch sensitivity, sight constriction and auras, vomiting, processing difficulties, and even language difficulties. It lasts hours. The worst one I've had sent me to the hospital for a nice stay that cost me a lot of money.

I didn't feel pain yet but it was coming. I struggled to drive straight but I knew I had to get home because of the time rush and I didn't want to be stranded on the road with a migraine. I'd push on as long as I could.

Aside from my physical battle, a spiritual and emotional war was raging too, a three front war that tested my resolve. My physical battle was enduring my symptoms with two and a half hours of night driving ahead. My spiritual front was attacked by a darkness that tested my boundaries. My thoughts went back to the day before and losing power to my legs and all of the strange thoughts that came with that. It was a real struggle inside not to think of all of the things it could have been that caused it.

Is this a migraine or is it more? Am I sick? Is it bad? How bad? Is it going to feel as bad as this? Am I going to die? We all die. I will die at some point. Is that sooner rather than later?

Thinking about the steps I needed to take when I got home got me scared. Call the doctor, get tested, find out what's wrong; OK, but I needed to get home first. I called out to God to help me get home. I prayed for my life so I wouldn't die driving on the road that night and so that I wouldn't die from some disease in my head. All the while, something was telling me I was going to, that I wasn't good enough, that I didn't have what it took to get back home or even live beyond that. This was way beyond my normal thought process and it was crushing. I prayed harder and harder. I prayed in tongues for that strength to get back.

My emotions were being hammered. Everything was critical for me in that car. I felt like crying but didn't. I stopped for a short while to rest hoping it would help. It didn't, but I did receive a call from my brother Ryan, seeing if I was going to be home to watch Lost. I could have asked for help but I didn't. I didn't want to have to bother anyone to drive out hours to fetch me. I knew this was my fight. This was bigger than just a migraine. This had to be won. I felt that if I submitted, then I lost. At this point, if I had given up, I would have been broken as a man. I had to wrestle this and get control so I moved on.

The last twenty minutes were the worst. My body was screaming to stop. I can't explain the physical feeling but I was surprised I didn't even have the headache yet. It was a strange ethereal feeling of tension, fatigue, and confusion. My brain was crawling. I remember praying, "Jesus take the wheel," because I couldn't drive anymore. I pulled into a gas station with no more fuel inside me. Feeling terrible, I knew I had to make a choice: stop here and give up or press the last few miles home. I turned the ignition on again and finished up.

I got home around 2:30a.m. and collapsed in my bed at the apartment. I woke up at 3:00a.m. to the headache and heaves. I had to be back at work early the next morning; throwing in the towel, I called in sick.

The next day was a day of healing from the weekend and the drive back. I felt victorious knowing I didn't break. I didn't give up. I was good enough. I will live.

Matt Maher had a concert that day up at St. Greg's. I made the effort to get there. I was still worn, weak, and weary from the episode. The migraine still echoed on. I saw some friends there but I couldn't explain what had happened. My soul needed healing. During the concert I reflected over the events that challenged me. I remembered the scripture I read from <u>Wild at Heart</u> and remembered going back to it when I was driving.

"Be strong and very courageous... Have I not commanded you? Do not be terrified; do not be discouraged, for the Lord your God will be with you wherever you go."

He made me strong enough. I am strong enough. Thank you Lord.

March 3, 2011

I went to see Narnia: Voyage of the Dawn Treader tonight with Jeremy, Mike, and Jamie. Lord, You have an amazing way of reaching me. The character of Aslan is a fantastic image of You. Tonight was awesome. The movie reminded me of my relationship with You. Actually, now that I think of it, the other movies (coming from the books) have a building effect to this point. I didn't feel this way when I saw the other movies, they were kind of a child's fantasy.

On my way home and continuing after walking through the door, I had a lovely talk with You, a reflection of recent worries. I've been stressed about where my life is going. But tonight, I feel at ease Lord. I prayed about my family and I asked that You keep us safe and healthy. Keep us together and keep us strong.

I prayed for my wife. I'll keep fighting for her. I don't even know her yet, but I love her. My heart has been unsettled because of the priesthood. But tonight, I feel as though You've broken me through this discernment to strengthen my heart for her. I serve You Lord, I gave You my life to do Your will, but I'll keep praying for a life partner, for her.

You sent the Spirit's gift on me tonight of joy and tears. Thank You. I love You and serve You.

Your humble (sometimes) servant,
Adam

◆

The Start of Full Time Ministry

God has a funny way of using us when we make ourselves available. When you say "yes", He uses you. He was teaching me to say "yes" all along the way. In hindsight, Luke 16:10 comes to mind, "He who is trustworthy in very small matters is also trustworthy in great ones; and the person who is dishonest in very small matters is also dishonest in great ones."

Up to this point, ministry was always something I wanted to do to give back to the Church. I had great role models in ministry who needed help and I always said, "yes" to more. When asked to help with teens for the first time, I said "yes". When asked to go to volunteer trainings, I said "yes". When asked to go on big trips, I said "yes". When called to help out more as a paid assistant, I said "yes". When I felt called to break the ice with young adult ministry for the first and second time, I said "yes".

It's not like I wasn't busy either. All the while, I was going to school full time and working full time, in addition to working unpaid internships; I gave more because I was called to. I knew God needed help. So He helped prepare me with every job I took on. Every experience that came my way, every class I took, I knew I was being formed. Into what? I thought I knew or at least hoped that I'd be planning events and menus for somebody and down the road, be running solo.

Then something interesting happened. I got a call to move for more and in a totally different direction. Or was it? All I could do is say…

◆

August 6 2012

Lord, You work in some pretty awesome and baffling ways. Joe got a job with Life Teen as East Coast Director and this is no doubt Your blessing on him and his family. You've moved him to a place where he can make a major difference for You.

What's really interesting is how You replaced him at St. Greg's with me. Joe and I were out at Mighty Taco for lunch when he mentioned how one day he will have to leave St. Greg's and will need a replacement. Casually, Joe asked me if I would do it. I said sure, thinking this is a joke. Little did I know…

Being fed up with the Olive Garden, I put my resume together (for the one hundredth time) to send out and upgrade jobs. I applied to a number of jobs including social media, hospitality, and event positions. However, UB was looking for a campus minister, which I decided to throw my hat in for. I put together a separate resume for ministry work and gave it to Joe to get his feedback. After using his recommendations, I sent my resume in. However, You had something else in mind.

After this, Joe told me that he got the job at Life Teen and that he recommended me for the job as youth minister at St. Greg's!

OK. Great. It meant a lot to me that Joe would think that highly of me to recommend me for the job. However, realistically, I had a snowball's chance in hell of getting it. At this point, I have an Associate's degree in Hospitality Management and I am working on my BS in Marketing and Entrepreneurship. No Theology. I have been involved in ministry for years, but as a volunteer. I spent a year as an assistant and running middle school ministry but that was just side work to help out. Plus, this is St. Greg's. They could get anyone they wanted. Nationally. No way I should get this.

Yet again, You work in mysterious ways. I went all in and just said "yes." For some reason, You want me here. I don't feel like I deserve to be here. There are so many people more qualified than me to fill the role. But. You put me here. I pray that You let me be the best I can be, that I step up to the plate and work hard for You. Guide me though perils and snares so I may lead others as You want me to.

I haven't started yet and I have to slow down in school. I feel like I'm in limbo but I trust You with this open door. By the sheer fact that I got the job, amongst so many odds shows me that You want this. Thank You. You are amazing.

August 6, 2012

So Lord, I feel a pretty amazing lesson has been taught to me. I think this is what I learned...

Working at the Olive Garden has given me many opportunities to date. After Lilly, I said, "I will never date another Olive Garden girl." And I have done well by that. No offense to Lilly, she's a great girl, but work relationships are complicated. I don't want to deal with that again. That was 2010 and today in 2012 I have never dated another OG girl since. Then Shawna walks in. Gorgeous brunette, lively, funny, You know... catches my eye. As I get to know her, she has a sad story. Turns out, she's early in a pregnancy and her "man" leaves her. She's a really special girl and certainly doesn't deserve that.

One day after work, I join up with a few co-workers for drinks. The conversation turns about Shawna. I remember saying that whoever that guy was really didn't know what he had. Shawna is the kind of girl you marry on the spot, not run away from. Anyways, Christina stopped the conversation and said that she thought I was in love with Shawna. That was ridiculous. I only knew her from the conversation we had at work. You can't fall in love with someone like that.

Yet the more I thought about it, I did find myself caring for her. Maybe a little crush. Well Christina made a case for me to pursue Shawna. I warmed up to the idea even though, at this point, a kid is on the way. But realistically, this couldn't happen anytime soon. Right?

Enter Jenna. Dyngus Day 2012 at the Hearthstone Manor. I had some serious swag that night because no girl was out of reach. I danced with everyone. One resisted. Jenna. Tall, cute, curly redhead. Friend of Carly. After me asking all night and prodding from her friends, she finally went out and danced with me. Got her number and we went out the next week. Had a slow few months of dating her, getting to know her. It took time and unfortunately, I held her at arm's length. I didn't let her into my heart. I don't really know why I had walls up at the time but as that started to thaw and I got ready to introduce her to my family and friends, a peculiar thing happened.

Shawna wrote on my Facebook wall a cryptic message that she was leaving the OG. At this time, I was sick as a dog. Couldn't sleep because my throat was killing me. I saw her message at 4a.m. and responded immediately in a private message. I thought since I would never see her again, I'd tell her how I felt. So I told her that I thought she was special and wished her good luck in the future. I sent this hoping the best for her but not caring if she responded, as long as she knew what I had to say. So what, I'd never see her again. Yet, the reality was, I was still seeing Jenna. Shawna responded with a message of her own saying she felt the same way and wanted to get to know me better outside of work. This led to a series of messages back and forth which led me to a difficult question... Do I break up with Jenna for Shawna?

This question haunted me. I felt like it should be easy. But how does a man looking to do the right thing answer this? Do I go for the girl I've had a connection with for some time and missed the boat or do I stand by the girl that I'm seeing now and defend her from competition?

I prayed that I may make the right decision. However, I feel like I didn't. I broke up with Jenna, really at the height of our relationship, without mentioning Shawna. As I sat and talked with her, I could see the heartbreak. During our conversation, I could feel like I was making a bad decision. It broke my heart too. After I left her place, I knew I screwed it up. I didn't break up with Jenna because I was ready to, but because I was greedy and wanted something better.

That something better turned out to be a mirage. The next day, a date I had set up with Shawna was canceled along with a note saying she wasn't ready for anything because of the kid at home.

So I failed the test. If that's what this was. I learned my lesson that I need to go up to bat for the woman at my side and be faithful. Be honest with her and block out the competition. Be a man with honor and dignity. Treat them the same. If the relationship isn't worth fighting for, it's OK to end it there and not drag it on, but don't muddle it.

Lord, I don't know how this will all work out but thank You for instilling this lesson on my heart. Help me to be a better man. Help Jenna and Shawna find good men who will be better than me.

January 5, 2013
The First Few Months in Ministry

So here I am Lord, on my fifth month as a youth minister. I am currently on the Core Retreat. Lord, this job is harder than I imagined. I feel like I'm not cut out for this. I feel like I just don't have the knowledge for it. It seems like everything I do is met with defeat or every victory comes at a steep cost. It's a struggle. I'm reeling right now with the Core's opinion of me: "Not being authentic," is uniquely hurtful. I don't know the source of that but it doesn't matter. I don't know what else I can do. I guess I'll just keep giving myself until you open another door or I fail out and they fire me. I don't think You put me here to do that though. I know I don't like to fail, who does? I press on... I love You. Thank you for trials and growth.

◆

St. Gregory the Great is the largest parish in the Buffalo Diocese. Knowing the reputation as an outsider, it's considered a monster. Over eighty ministries and over fifteen thousand people were registered upon my arrival. It was difficult to relate to any other parish I've had exposure to. Our pastor who hired me had been well established and liked there. This was a man running the ship with confidence. He had the parish running like a well-oiled machine, tuned-up for his system. Unfortunately, I was a different gear installed into that system: a Ford part in a Chevrolet engine.

I inherited one of the best run youth ministries in Buffalo. With flourishing high school and middle school programs, St. Greg's Youth Ministry was on fire. Also unique to St. Greg's, was the fact that there were two full time youth ministers, an unheard-of investment by a parish in Buffalo. Upon my arrival, I found things to be more difficult than I ever would have imagined. Under the hood, I found a disdain for the change from what was—from our volunteers, teens, parents, and even staff. Conscious of what making major changes would do to an organization, I mostly plugged into what was already in motion. While it's hard to gauge in hindsight what a different route would have cost me, I paid a tough toll to cross the bridge.

Still being green at the full-time effort, compounded by an organization resistant to change, I found myself swimming hard early. A couple months after being hired, my partner in middle school left to do ministry at her home parish. So, any stability from having her carry through the transition was gone. The teens and the Core Team volunteers rebelled. Trying to bring in fresh faces to a going deeper night called FBI, I found them chased away by the handful of kids already there. A couple of them even pulled me aside and said, "This is our Jesus club Adam, we don't want anyone else here."

In the rebellion, kids would go nuts during our gatherings by jumping on and over couches and furniture. They would run to the café freezer and pull out whatever they wanted and eat it.

I won't ever forget one kid (who later became a ministry victory by hiring him) decided it would be a good idea to pull out a giant tub of cookie dough from the café freezer. I caught him strolling into our night like a boss, one arm shoving a spoon halfway down his throat and the rest of the tub under the other.

Even trying to bring in new volunteers was a problem. A new Core Member who quit shortly after joining the team told me, "I'm not welcome here. I can't do it. I don't fit in with them."

At a Core Meeting, a couple of the established Core Members told me tongue-in-cheek, "You have a full team of youth ministers here Adam; any one of us can do this." Gossip was thick too. I heard the echoes of it every day. I wasn't Joe and some on the team were just waiting for me to quit.

These instances were not even breaking into the surface. I told myself from the beginning that I didn't sign up for easy. Every day proved that right. While pushed to my limits, often wrestling with the temptation to throw in the towel, I didn't quit when it got hard. I prayed and worked harder. Thank God.

◆

November 16, 2013
Fall Confirmation Retreat

> It has been some time since I last wrote. We've come a long way. We've turned the corner with the ministry, Your ministry. I'm on the Fall Confirmation Retreat at Camp Turner. We have a great crew with us here. I love You Lord and thank You for Your presence here in this place. Thank you for Your help and love.

I still feel a pull on my heart. I'm not settled here...yet. I don't feel at home even though we got through some of the worst mess and started repairing the broken relationships and the organization. We turned the corner but I can't help the feeling that this isn't supposed to be my main breadwinner. What's next Lord? Help me get there. I know You will and I trust You. In other news, thank you for Ani. Help me be a better man for her. Help me to soften my heart for her. In related thoughts, help me to prepare for my wife. Whoever she may be.

March 29, 2014
Spring Retreat: "Sent"
7:35a.m.

We're at the Seminary this weekend for the High School Retreat: "Sent". A lot of time went into planning this retreat but I feel like I have no idea what I'm doing. I'm a wee- bit tired today but that's how it goes. I think we have a great group of teens and Core members with us and I'm looking forward to the rest of the retreat. We had a couple of hiccups but we rolled on. I'm ready for anything at this point.

March 30, 2014
Spring Retreat "Sent"
7:53a.m.

Whew, this retreat was hard. Of course the Ghost of Christmas Past shows up, Fr. Tom. Why did we come to the Seminary again? No big deal right? Just let it roll off. One word has been hitting me lately and especially last night in Adoration: abdicate. With already being stretched thin, I can't give anymore than I already am. There is so much to do that there is a sense of being underwater. I'm not being successful at this over-fulltime work and fulltime school. I should gear down. There are gaps in my school work and in my job. At least with work, maybe someone better can take my place.

I feel that this pace is unhealthy. Relationships and mental health are taking hits. Looking for an open door.

May 3, 2014
Christian Music Summit
9:50a.m.

Currently at the Christian Music Summit. Feeling on the cusp of leaving St. Greg's. Lord, I don't know if You're calling me for further beatings in ministry at SGYM or a restart on a new opportunity. There is a lot of tension with this. I'm currently hearing that I should be satisfied in You. Help me to be satisfied in You and where You are taking me. I want to walk whatever that road is, just help me to be tough enough, strong enough, smart enough.

July 7, 2014
Covecrest
7:46a.m.

It's been six years since I first wrote in this book on my first trip to Covecrest. Six years of growing with You. Six years of learning what it means to trust in You. I am here along the lake in the morning. Steam is rising from the water, the sun is rising over the tree line, birds are chirping, and a bullfrog is croaking. It's a beautiful sight.

Lord, this trip is straining on me. It was a disaster to pull together and there is no way I could have done it without You. In fact, the only way I could have done it is with You. Every twist and turn was one challenge or another. You had to drag me to the finish line on this one. As messy as it was, thanks for letting me run the race.

... I was just interrupted by Jeremy and it was nice to have a morning heart to heart about struggles in ministry. Thanks again for training by fire.

July 9, 2014
Covecrest
7:10 a.m.

Lord, I have spent a lot of time writing in this book about my future wife. Thanks for putting that on my heart and for letting my heart grow and mature. You've taught me so much with being with Ani. I have a new appreciation for chastity and I believe that struggle has given our relationship depth. Thanks for teaching me not to worry about superficial things. Every time I seek a way out over something stupid, You heal a corner of my heart. I hear You when I'm ignorant. You've given me an answer about her when I need one. Ani is so easy going and straightforward yet You've been unlocking and unveiling her heart every step of the way. Or maybe you're just opening up my own heart.

We've just reached our one-year-anniversary on the 4th and what a year it has been. Leaving her this week had made me experience for the first time in a long time, unreserved love. I miss her and long to see her again. Her heart is pure and she knows what she wants. Lately, we've been talking about a future together: marriage, house, kids. I think my heart has finally begun to prepare for that. There are a lot of challenges to overcome. Time and finances need to be taken care of. I have little money to get a place of my own let alone pay for a ring, wedding, honeymoon, house, life...

I trust You that this will work out. If she is the one, it'll happen.

July 9, 2014
Covecrest
7:20a.m.

I'm currently in the chapel for my penance from when I went to confession the other day during our time in the lake. It was pretty cool to have priests floating in life jackets in the water. I just had to swim out there. I've never seen that before. Wild. So I went to a priest I never met before and didn't catch his name. I got through two confessions that were at the top of my list. 1. My struggle to achieve chastity in my relationship with Ani. 2. Fatigue and failing to trust You in my placement at St. Greg's.

The priest told me to get a spiritual director about my second confession. I don't know if my sustained restlessness at St. Greg's is a call to perseverance or if it's a call out. So far it's been the former but this coming year will tell. I go back to school to finish what I started at Canisius. I cringe at the thought of doing school and Greg's again after taking a year off. I wait for You to find an open door for me or to help me find joy in what I'm doing.

Help me to be the best that I can be at whatever I do.

July 9, 2014
Covecrest
10:55p.m.

We had Adoration tonight in the main room. A great peace came into my heart tonight as I walked around the room. All of the teens were focused on You as our hour and a half together progressed.

Leading up to Exposition, Joe told his story of how he met his wife, Kelly, and how they came to be married. They trust You with everything and know You will provide, and look at the blessings You've poured down on them. Did I decide tonight to marry Ani? Lord, I wait for confirmation.

Just a pause from the direct journal, this would be the first time I seriously entertained the thought. It would take me a year to wrestle it out, plan, and save but for the first time I opened the door to marriage with Ani. I still didn't know if marriage was what God wanted of me but there was a decision to be made. Enter "Operation Elephant", my code name for the proposal, an uncertain journey that would require more than just a plan, it would require everything I have and more.

July 11, 2014

Am I taking advantage of all the available opportunities that God had blessed me with? Have I said "yes" to them? Am I giving my all or my best?

Lord, this is the last day at camp! While I was expecting a re-charge or reboot for youth ministry, I can't help but feel fatigued about what's next. Help rest my heart and let me find peace in my work. Help me to have satisfaction in You. Help me to find joy in my labor as You use me to do Your will.

July 26, 2014
Core Retreat, Camp Pioneer

I thank You for such an awesome woman. Ani and I had a difficult evening the other day. We screwed up and stumbled in our battle for chastity. This spurred a challenge for us. You made us better than that. She's a beautiful woman who deserved better from me. She wanted to take the blame for herself but it takes two to tango. We're a team and we're in it together. Here are a few text messages from her after the fact…

> "I know we may be weak in the moment, but you are the strong faithful man I have always prayed for."
>
> "We can do this! But not on our own"
>
> "So I wanna make a commitment to you and to God to be persistent in prayer and my intentions about this!"
>
> Ani, July 25, 2014

What a woman! What a challenge. What a blessing.

Lord I want to be a better man for You, for her, and for myself. Help me to lead the dance. Help me to lead her to Heaven. Help us live a more holy relationship. Help me to love more fully, not lustfully.

She has such a pure heart and I want to contribute to that, not ruin it.

> "I want us to build each other up in faith and keep each other on a righteous path."
>
> Ani, July 25, 2014

Scripture from our conversation:

1 Corinthians 13; Genesis 1&2; Song of Songs.

> "The first line of that famous scripture is 'love is patient'. We need to be patient, we will have our time but how much more special that will be if we are patient now and wait until we are joined together as one in the sacrament of marriage?"
>
> Ani, July 25, 2014

Right on Girl, right on.

The only way we can do this Lord is in You. I give our relationship to You and may our hearts rest in You. May our love reflect Your own.

July 27, 2014
Core Retreat, Camp Pioneer

Lord, I'm sitting on the beach in reflection, hearing the waves come ashore. One of the biggest questions on my heart is: Where do I go from here? Am I taking advantage of all of the opportunities You've given me?

Is Righteous Co. a thing? Is there something around the corner? Do I stay at St. Greg's? How long? Can You make it work? I feel empty and burned out by staying. What's the next open door?

Questions for you:

1. Are you taking advantage of all the opportunities around you right now? Why or why not?

2. What are the opportunities you are tapping into? Are you giving them your best? Pursuing excellence?

3. What are the opportunities you have not tapped into? Why haven't you? What fears keep you sidelined?

4. What are the ones out of reach?

5. What is your dream? Is God a part of that dream?

Challenges:

- Take your dreams to prayer. Whatever you are shooting for, ask God into it. Listen to see if it's where He wants you to go. Be patient. Understand you may or may not be doing what He's intended.

- Go to an Adoration chapel, remove your inner distractions, and just listen for the Lord for an hour.

If you know the enemy and know yourself, your victory will not stand in doubt; if you know Heaven and know Earth, you may make your victory complete.

SUN TSU

CHAPTER THREE

The Hammer

"How is it that iron sharpens iron?" the apprentice asked. Striking the glowing-hot metal the master responded, "This hammer has already been refined of impurities and was made strong," and pounded again. "The ore was prepared well to do its job. Every hammer strike calls out what could weaken your metal. It takes heat and pressure," another strike. "Resilience and strength," strike. "Patience and fortitude," strike. "Only then, can the iron be strong enough to form another." The master paused and looked intently at the apprentice, "As I am the master, the hammer," another strike, "You are the student, the ore."

◆

Heat is only a part of the formation process. A blacksmith will use many tools for the job at hand but the iconic hammer and anvil is a mainstay. Not only will the directed and intentional strikes give form to the glowing element, it now makes it possible to jettison the impurities from the metal for good.

If you've seen heat and hammer, what form has been taken shape for you?

◆

August 4 & 12, 2014
Home and Confirmation Retreat

I met with Fr. Marty last week for spiritual advisement. I think he is the smartest and wisest man I know. With the recent turmoil on my heart and at St. Greg's, I really needed to talk to someone that could guide me. Thanks for opening the door for me to link up with him. I've known him for a long time and it's been a long road to get to this point with him. I'm glad he's my first spiritual advisement.

It was great catching up with him but the real meat and potatoes came with his help with discerning Your will. My problem up to this point is that I've been waiting for You to open doors for me, sitting, mostly impatiently and restless for things to happen. Fr. Marty shared with me his discernment process for the priesthood. He shared how he asked, "What should I do?" while on his 30 day retreat and nothing happened. He asked again, "What should I do?" to which nothing happened. Then he asked, "Are You there Lord?" and You responded, "Yes, I'm here."

So he asked again, "Well, what should I do?"

Silence.

Franticly, "Are You there?"

THE HAMMER

"Yes, I'm here."

Searching for an answer, "Well, what should I do?"

The Lord's response was, "Well, what do you want to do?"

He made the point that honed my view on Your will. We have to choose. You're in our desires and dreams. We shouldn't be afraid to dream. I shouldn't be afraid to dream or to act or make decisions. I feel like this is a new level of faith. One where I can't sit on my hands and wait for You to move. This is a level where I take responsibility for my life and actions and allow You to work in my decisions and dreams. This is more difficult to swallow because I need to be decisive and that requires greater faith in You. As Fr. Marty put it, like a trapeze artist letting go of one swing, trusting that the next one is there to catch. Or, how Peter could have walked out on water even though logically it didn't make sense. I feel like I'm Peter in the boat and Jesus saying, "Come, step in the water and keep your eyes on me."

"You need endurance to do the will of God and receive what he promised." Hebrews 10:36

"For I know well the plans I have for you says the Lord, plans for your welfare, not for woe, plans to give you a future full of hope. When you call me, when you go to pray to me I will listen to you." Jeremiah 29: 11-13

"Come"[...] "O you of little faith, why did you doubt me?" Matthew 14:22-33

August 19, 2014
Young Christians at Work

Well Lord, one more year.

This is me letting go of the trapeze, getting out of the boat in the storm.

One more year. One more year of SGYM and school. I risk failing either or both. I thought I have known the bottom of the tank and I'm sure I'll be challenged beyond that. I may have to dig deeper than ever. I will. Help me to dig in. Give me my shield, sword, helmet, and spear.

I trust You.

While my batteries are shot and the road broken, I trust that You'll be my energy, my strength, my courage, endurance, light, and fire. Make me tenacious, fearless, bold, and strong.

"I am strong enough."

Please give me rest when I need it. When I hit my low, give me hope. Protect my heart, body, and soul.

I don't know what the next pages hold but I pray not only that I do I not fail, but also that I flourish, that we flourish and find victory.

In Your name I pray and work, live and love.

October 7, 2014

St. Greg's brought in Jason Evert to speak on chastity yesterday. I was fortunate enough to have dinner with him and some of the staff before driving him back to the church to prepare. He shared some awesome tips but the real blessing was hearing his talk. It was just what the doctor ordered to recharge the batteries. The fight for purity in mind, soul, and body is tough and there comes a point when you lose sight of what and who you are fighting for.

Lord, I fight for You, for the beautiful woman You sent me, for the people I lead (or don't), and for myself.

"Love alone is worth the fight."—Switchfoot

Thanks for the recharge.

October 8, 2014 – 8th Grade Retreat, CTK Seminary

Currently in Adoration with the 8th grade at the Seminary. This week is nuts...

SUN	MON	TUE	WED - THU	FRI-SUN
JRev (HS Teen Night)	Jason Evert	Man Class (HS Guy Night)	8th Grade Retreat	Eucharistic Teen Retreat

Plus

School work each day.

Lord I trust You. I need You in this.

Fr. Leon did his meditation and asked us to have a mantra...

Endurance, strength

Endurance, strength

Endurance, strength

November 15, 2014
Confirmation Retreat, CTK Seminary
11:50p.m.

Back at the Seminary again on the third Confirmation Retreat this year with Fr. Leon. We're in Adoration again and again my mantra is "endurance".

I'm feeling fatigued right now in ministry and school. The semester is long and hard and I'm winded. I'm at risk of failing two classes in my second last semester which is causing me some anxiety. I turn 30 on Monday, which is no problem but it does mark the end of an age.

Lord, I trust You. Help me to dig deep and drive forward. This is tough stuff. To walk on water, I can't flinch. Help me to keep my eyes on You in the storm. Help me to not be afraid and doubtful.

On another note, Ani put together an awesome surprise party for me. I don't think I've ever had one before. She didn't have to do that, but hey, it was adorable. I was happy to see everyone. Thank you for family, friends, and especially her.

Bring on the 30's.

In other news, big changes at St. Greg's. There has been an exodus of staff members since the transition to Fr. Leon. This marks the end of the Fr. Tom era. One I was a stranger to. It's interesting to see Your works through this. Every reason for me leaving is being addressed: the leadership, volunteer problems, the basement renovation; can I support a family? Can I find joy in my work?

November 17, 2014
3:45 a.m.

Lord, I just turned 30. It's my birthday. It's almost 4am and I am on my bedroom floor looking at the board Ani made for me. It's a collage of pictures and cutouts from my life. I sit here and look at this board with nostalgia and love. Ani has worked so hard on this. It shows the amount of care and craft she put into it. She must have gone through a lot of pictures because she picked out some good B sides. Baby, childhood, high school, family, Life Teen, paintball, Tough Mudder, Germany, Italy, kayaking, sacraments, and even a corner made with pictures of the two of us.

She has worked hard to make this birthday the best I ever had. She set up a surprise birthday party on Friday, which was awesome; it was great to see everyone. She revealed later that it was supposed to be on Saturday at the Casino at Chestnut Ridge Park. It fell through because

I was on retreat. She wouldn't tell me how much she lost on the deposit. I feel bad about that... whoops.

For all that she has done, I gave little more than a "thank you". For a guy who has been enjoying the moment and smelling the roses, I almost let this one go by without notice. I'm really glad that I am taking the time to reflect right now. This is a woman who loves me deeply and I am letting her slip by without the support, encouragement, the recognition, and the love she deserves. This is what it means to love. Where the tire hits the road. Showing appreciation for her. Letting her know and see what she means to me.

Recalling what she said at dinner at the party, "Why aren't you spending time with me?" She said it in a way that felt hurt or abandoned. Thinking about it, I was really spending time with everyone else and wasn't paying her any attention. On Friday at the Armor Inn she said something similar, "you're spending time with everyone but me." Not in a demanding or belittling way, but in a way of longing and desire. A way that says, "I just want to be with you. I made this for you and I just want you to notice."

Come on me. This beautiful woman is a gift. I need to do better and make sure I notice that she wants to be loved in return. Show it. Don't miss opportunities to love her even in the little ways. Strengthen her, don't leave her disappointed. While she would never say that, I should know it. I know it's busy but make the time.

Babe, I love you and appreciate all that you do. Someday soon I will make it loud and clear in a life changing way.

Reflecting on my past 30 years, I appreciate all of the blessings and challenges I've had. Family, friends, job and learning experiences, childhood memories, trips around the country and to Europe, old girlfriends, victories, failures, hopes and dreams.

To quote a sticker on Ani's board, "Love this life". Yes I do.

Thank you Lord for these 30 years. I pray that You continue to bless me as I move forward. Help me to love better, to grow further, and serve You better with my life. Continue to teach me and keep my family and I healthy and free from catastrophe. I love You and trust You.

P.S. Ani has a surprise for me later today. I will be sure to tell her my appreciation and love for her. (3 days of Ani lovin)

December 12, 2014
Canisius College Chapel

It's the last day of classes for the hardest semester of my life so far. It has been a hard and difficult road getting here. I've struggled through accounting and calculus. I was afraid of failing but I've trusted You along the way. One moment was especially hard when my stress was inescapable. I was walking to class close to despair with what seemed like the weight of the world, but then I had a thought. That no matter what, You are with me, even if I fail. I knew that even in failure I should keep my head high, like a proud soldier of the gentleman age, surrendering to an adversary. That nipped the fear dead, there isn't anything to be afraid of here.

So I put my head high and kept on to class, not to surrender, but to keep fighting because failure here isn't the end. So fight I did. Now I'm winning. Lesson? I won't give up even when victory seems impossible. I will take it to the end and keep my head high no matter the outcome because whatever the outcome is, it's not worth despairing over. There is something to be said about the ferocity gained when close to defeat. If I give in before the battle is done, then I lose the opportunity to use that edge to get it done.

I know You are there and I should be proud of my best. One more semester to go.

December 15, 2014
The Man Closet (New, Smaller, Apartment)

Lord, help me prepare my heart, energy, time, and soul to my new ministry of marriage and family with Ani. I've been feeling dissonance on my heart and feeling down. Thanks for the boost.

Last night we went out with Fr. Dave for drinks and wings. It was awesome to tell our story. It was important for me to do so. He asked us each why we love the other. It was beautiful to think about, hear, and verbalize.

What am I preparing for? I can choose my direction but I need to put the time and effort into it. The time and thought I put into my job and ministry is consuming. Can I imagine if I put the same amount into my family? Can I imagine "big picture family" like I can imagine "big picture church"?

January 17, 2015
Confirmation Retreat, Christ the King Seminary

It's the last Confirmation Retreat for the year and I am again in the chapel at St. Paul's dorm, in front of You in the Eucharist. The past week has been really interesting, no, make that the last month. Jen and I received new job descriptions. I'm now in charge of youth ministry, high school and middle school. Two jobs, one man. Jen moves to young adults.

While I should be use to gut shots, this one sure takes the wind out of me. There is tremendous opportunity with the new direction but, there is also an equal amount of weight to go with it. Fr. Leon wants big stuff to happen. I agree. However, we just stopped the requirement for Confirmation students to attend JRev and the numbers went from 50-100 to 8. On opening night we had three of the eight teens plus a Core member leave. Bailed. Scrammed. Total disappointment.

I now have to rebuild two programs, Edge and Life Teen mid-year; each is a fulltime job here. Plus, I have to have greater presence into all of the youth activities/groups in the parish: Choirs, school, ski club, sacristans, altar servers, boy scouts, Don Bosco and St. Bernadette's clubs, plus Family Faith Formation and who knows what else. Daunting. Winded.

Fr. Leon wants a reboot of sorts for youth ministry. I'm fatigued already and worn thin. I hope that this is Your move and that You will provide blessings. I hope this is the tearing down of obstacles because Lord, this could easily destroy me unless it's from You.

Help us to restructure so we can have a healthy community and lead the most teens and young adults to You. Let St. Greg's be the best it can be plus more. With or without me. If this is for me, then I accept. If it's meant for my replacement, then I thank You. I would like to offer up my prayer for the youth of the parish and pray that St. Greg's becomes a fortress for You to lead from. Build a spiritual army and nation from here. Take back the world!

January 20, 2015
Spot Coffee

I'm at Spot Coffee right now with the intent to read scripture. I'm using a Bible study from one of the companies we subscribe to. It matches up songs with the readings and topics. Kinda cool. The topic for today, "God's presence" and the song is "Blessed Assurance" by Elevation Worship. Neat.

1 Peter 5:7 – "Cast all of your anxiety on Him because He cares for you."

Hebrews 13:8 – "Jesus Christ is the same yesterday, today, and forever."

Blessed Assurance – "This is my story, this is my song, praising my Savior all the day long."

February 25, 2015
The Man Closet

I went out tonight with Dan for a couple of beers and to catch up on life. We started off with small talk but we got on the topic of our significant others. I opened up to him about how things are going with Ani and shared my witness about my journey with You that led me to Ani. Strangely enough, he had a similar story of coming to You to ask for Your daughter's hand in marriage.

Lord, I've been so on fire for Ani. Every day I find that I desire her more and more. I'm falling in love with her even more. It's 92 days until Operation Elephant. I can't wait. Thank you for prepping my heart for her. Thank you for walking alongside us in our fight for purity. I truly believe this struggle to build discipline is what will get me to the finish line with her.

To the mountaintop. This journey is like climbing a mountain. It seems easy on TV but until you do it, you just don't realize the difficulty or what goes into it. I love You Lord and I love her. I also pray that her tests go well…

March 18, 2015
Youth Office, St. Greg's

Today has been a rough day. I'm three days away from the high school Spring Retreat and I'm feeling pretty beat up. I felt like I did a good job yesterday, regrouping and charging up. However, Fr. Ben bailed on us last minute. It doesn't look like we'll have a replacement. No Confession, no Benediction, and no Mass. This is the second time this year a priest bailed on me last minute for a retreat. I'm pissed. It's on days like this that I can't wait to be done with Youth Ministry. The abrasions never end.

Mom was in the hospital this week for a scare that ended up being a muscle spasm and she had her first reconstructive surgery in her battle against breast cancer. Please return her to good health. Help her to heal and be a confident warrior again for You.

In other news, I'm reflecting on an earlier conversation with an adorable little girl with Down Syndrome who saw a picture of Ani and said, "Mary! Mary!" it melted my heart that she would be reminded of Mary when she saw her. Talking with her mom, it was clarified that she was saying, "Marry! Marry!" Then the little girl said "Bride! Bride!"

I think it's funny how she called that out just from the picture on my screen. Yes Molly, I will marry her and yes she will be my bride. She just doesn't know that for sure yet. Thanks Lord.

THE HAMMER

March 21, 2015
Spring Retreat: "The Brick", Camp Turner

Well Lord, here I am on the Spring Retreat. So far so good. It's journal time but I don't think many are taking it seriously. It's OK, there will be time later for them to work on it.

This week has been tough. Hell has been against us but thanks for prevailing. I was furious that Fr. Ben bailed. I can't remember the last time I was that angry.

Then You covered my back and blessed us with a priest. Fr. Marty was available and was willing to come. The hats were finished on time and we got everyone here safe and sound. Thanks. Please continue to bless this retreat and open the hearts of everyone here.

> "The Spirit of the Lord God is upon me, because the Lord has anointed me; He has sent me to bring good news to the afflicted, to bind up the broken hearted, to proclaim liberty to captives, release to the prisoners." Isaiah 61:1

Journal question—Where do you need Christ to bring you freedom in your life?

*I paused on answering this question earlier... Now I'm in Adoration.

Lord, I'm not sure where I need freedom. A part of me wants to be free from St. Greg's. While it is a blessing in my life, it's also a huge burden, a cross. Maybe it's my perception but I don't feel joy in this. Like a stranger in a foreign land. The lows are low. I think I'm ready for a new opportunity but as with everything, please help me to endure through the difficulty. Help me see the joy.

We watched a video with Mark Hart about Your passion and death. Awful. Gruesome. If being put through the ringer here is the least I can do for You, then so be it. I know nothing I can do can repay You, except to give You my heart. So I endure.

April 7, 2015
The Man Closet

Good morning Lord. This Lent has been a struggle for me. I was unfocused in my sacrifices. I gave up the usual lusting, attempted to go to daily Mass once a week, but most of all I wanted to use this time as preparation for marriage.

I maybe went to daily Mass once. Did OK with dealing with lust but Ani and I have been working on that since before Lent, so it seemed disconnected. And I did nothing for the preparation for marriage.

My mind has been on overdrive and I could not for the life of me stay committed to any of them. It's two days after Easter and I see the lesson You're giving me. While I failed at daily Mass and floated through lust, You certainly have been preparing my heart for marriage.

THE HAMMER

Ani and I have been struggling, whether she knows it or not. I suspect she does. I think we're both tired and fatigued at where we are. Me at St. Greg's and school, her working three jobs. We barely see each other. Date nights on Mondays usually end up being stay-in nights because we're too tired to go out. She has been cranky and kind of bossy and I guess I have been too. Either way, she's been annoying me with her lack of communication when she gets into bad moods.

I think the little things add up. Small slights, little recognition and communication, a touch of life stress, and a cup of fatigue have created this cake we've been eating and it's a poisonous cake.

I thought about this in the shower yesterday. I thought about why it's happening. I thought about how to fix it. Maybe I'm not correctly communicating what I want. Maybe I need to be tougher and stronger with her. Maybe she just isn't the one and I should start over (OK it crossed my mind but I didn't spend a lot of time on that).

Then I realized that this is my preparation. Marriage isn't all sunshine and lollypops. Sometimes it's just hard. Love is hard. Life is hard. My first response was that she just doesn't get it, I need to be harder on her, and maybe I should just walk away and find something better. None of these are compatible with love. I have the choice to pursue any option but I am designed for love and really the only option I need to choose is to be selfless. Just as

You showed on the Cross. Just how You lived down here with us. It always takes sacrifice.

While I wasn't able to achieve my preparation myself, You have been laying it out for me. You taught me to be selfless with body and now to be selfless of heart. Thank you, I love You, and I love her.

Continue to help me grow into a better man for her. Help me to live selflessly for her. Thank you for the lessons in perseverance. I am sure my training today will come in handy later.

◆

Operation Elephant was the product of a year's worth of prayer and planning. After making the decision at Camp Covecrest to pursue marriage with Ani, it all started to fall into place. I wanted to make a statement, a statement that said that I was serious about us and serious about marriage. I wanted to bring her back to where I made the decision; so I plotted out the course. Being from Buffalo, it isn't an easy sixteen-hour drive as a couple *striving* for chastity. So to make sure that we would be taking the trip right, I contacted my friends in the D.C. area to split the time. We would stay with them overnight with separate accommodations to save us from having to go the hotel route. It worked out great logistically but it was a pleasing bonus to be able to include them in the event. Taking the time to travel for fun isn't easy to do, so to be able to see my buddies created an excellent dynamic to the trip.

The next part of the trip to be hashed out was our stay in Georgia and visit to the camp. The way I had to convince Ani, as well as her parents, was to have a viable reason for such a trip without hinting at what I thought would be the obvious, a proposal. It just so happened that my friends Joe and Kelly and their family lived close to the camp. In my mind, he would be the perfect alibi. We did have a standing invite to visit after all. Moreover he worked for Life Teen and had pull for Covecrest.

I called Joe and explained my plans. Operation Elephant was now in effect. As time drew near and we solidified our plans to visit Joe and company, I was put on the spot by Ani's mom at dinner. With everyone there she proclaimed, "Now would be a great time to explain your intentions about this trip, Adam." I almost crapped my pants.

Apparently, I wasn't clear enough on our travel plans, but I felt like she also sensed something was up. At this point, we were months away from departure. I was planning on asking her dad for her hand but I wasn't ready for that. On the hot seat, I coolly emphasized that we would have appropriate lodging for the trip. This of course was a concern for good Italian parents. Then it was dropped. Either that was sufficient or they knew this was part of a bigger plan. I was relieved they didn't push further. Bullet dodged.

Next hurdle was to find the right ring. I had no idea where to begin. Starting with watching the history on why we use diamond rings for engagement, I wasn't sure I even wanted to go that route. That custom has a pretty short history and is the by-product of a marketing campaign by DeBeers. But a diamond is forever right?

I looked around at all the box stores, but I had no idea what I was looking at. I saw some designs I thought looked good but I didn't want to get something sitting on the shelf. The salespeople were less than helpful; it was as if I was buying candy. "Look at this lollipop, doesn't it look delicious? It's only $999.99. Should I bag it up?"

After thinking about it, I didn't want to short-change Ani. While I'm sure she would have been fine with a string, I know what the expectation is for everyone else. This was a once-in-a-lifetime opportunity. Didn't I want to make a statement? Yes. I wanted to go above her expectations. Plus, diamonds are appealing when thinking about what they represent. A well sought-out rock does matter. They are the strongest stones on record, nearly unbreakable. Their glow and clarity is unmatched. The way they catch and pass light captivates the eye like no other. The formation of a diamond requires a lot of heat and pressure over time and the circumstances and elements must be just right. Lastly, there is the task of finding the right one. It demands attention and care. There are a lot of rocks out there that are cheap cuts with suspicious histories.

I spoke with a friend of mine about the situation and he gave me the contact of a local jeweler he used for his engagement ring. I stopped to see Mark the owner of the shop and what a world of difference. As a geologist, he was well educated on the rocks. He handcrafted rings and used GIA certified stones. (Side-note gentlemen: Know the four C's when looking for a ring: carat, cut, clarity, color. You'll pay big bucks for the best in each category. Don't just go for the biggest carat. Find a well-rounded rock in your budget—but as Mark demonstrated, clarity gives a brilliance to the stone that is most appealing.)

Mark showed me the identification laser imprinted on the diamond itself through the microscope. He is a craftsman with a background in geology and takes great care of his work but most importantly, he is an honest man. He spent a lot of time with me and I never felt rushed. I returned a few times as he educated me on the range of diamonds and walked me through the four C scales. I got the confidence of what style I wanted and found the right stones to crown it, Mark began the work.

◆

May 27, 2015
One Day Before Operation Elephant

"It's almost show time," was a text message that I sent to Mark and Jamie. Tomorrow Ani and I will embark on our trip to Georgia. This is a trip of a lifetime. When we leave, it's the start of the rest of our lives together. I picked up the engagement ring earlier today. It's gorgeous. This ring is what I'm going to use to initiate our engagement, so much symbolism in that small piece of jewelry. Purity, clarity, strength, beauty, all forged into one ring.

I'm excited to propose to her. I'm excited to get the ball rolling. I'm excited to move forward with her. It has been a long road to get here. Lord, thank you for the lessons it took to get to this point. Thank you for teaching me how to love more fully; for teaching me what it means to be a man; for teaching me what it costs to give my heart to someone.

I pray for our trip, that it be everything it needs to be. That we are safe and that the start of our road to marriage honors You. Bless our family and let our children be Yours and healthy. Help us to prosper in all ways so we can serve You better.

I love You Lord and I love Your daughter Ani. Let's do this!

May 29, 2015 (Operation Elephant Day 2)
Joe and Kelly's, Marietta, Georgia

I'm sitting on Joe's couch before bed. It's been a long day of driving and I'm hungry and tired. I feel good though. This is the last night I'll be single. This point forward I'll be preparing for a wedding and marriage. I suspect Ani knows. Joe was originally going to join us at Covecrest but mentioned earlier today that he was going to stick home to be with his family before leaving for the Life Teen Convention. I get it but he was my alibi as to why we were even going to Covecrest. It made sense if he was inviting us but why would we drive another two hours after driving sixteen, to visit a camp? Yes, it's a cool camp, but why? I wonder if she's thinking it...

Lord I'm ready.

Questions for you

1. Do you have someone or something you are fighting for? Write out the battle. Who or what is it you're battling? Are you winning or losing? What is it going to take to win?

2. Who do you know that can back you up with prayer? Have you asked this person yet to do so?

3. Have you taken this battle to prayer? Have you offered it to God?

Challenges:

- Offer up your battles to God in your prayer time and start the road to 100% trust in Him. Write down the battlefield.

- Find a Spiritual Director. Go to your parish pastor or priest to recommend where to start.

*Act and
God will act.*

ST. JOAN OF ARC

CHAPTER FOUR

The Whetstone

The apprentice had come a long way in his learning. The master taught him many things in the trade. Hard learning took many forms from direct lessons to mistakes made but the apprentice persevered. Now that the student had many skills that formed the base of his knowledge, he was ready to hone his craft. The master was proud of him and was following along on a project the student was engaged with.

"That is an excellent blade," he said upon lifting the work, testing its balance. A resounding ting as he touched it with his finger announced its purity. The master reached into his apron, pulled out his cherished whetstone, and smiled, recalling many memories. He had used this whetstone to sharpen many blades and teach many apprentices in his seemingly countless years. He handed the apprentice the stone, "You have become a capable craftsman, and I am very proud of you."

After the design and form are completed, polish continues the process. Without it, instruments are not as effective for its purpose. Even after use, a blade can become dull and will need to be sharpened again to get back to top shape. Whetstones smooth out and sharpen blades—in what ways do you need polish?

◆

May 30, 2015 (Operation Elephant Day 3)
Joe and Kelly's, Marietta, Georgia

We're engaged! She said "yes"! Didn't doubt for a second that she would. Lord, thank you for every step to get us to this point. Today was amazing. It's liberating knowing the path ahead. I know my purpose and Vocation. My primary purpose is to lead Ani and our family to Heaven, to You. Help me to achieve this by giving me the wisdom to make the right decisions, the perseverance to get through the tough stuff, and the faith to always seek You.

Let me always offer my best for Ani and whatever family You bless us with. Years of screaming at the beach, fighting with You in the car, or just being stupid was really embarrassing. But, this is who I fought for. This is who I have prayed for and wondered about. I'm truly blessed and ready for this next chapter in the book of life. Now if we can do something about the career...

May 30, 2015 (Operation Elephant Day 3, Later)
Joe and Kelly's, Marietta, Georgia

Today was amazing and I'm wondering if I should write about the details or leave it to memory and pictures. I guess I'll write while it's fresh.

It was a beautiful day outside; low 80's, sunny, birds chirping, bees buzzing around the clovers. Covecrest was just as beautiful as I remembered it. The rolling greens hills, the lake, the camp dogs.

Because Joe couldn't be there, a friend of his showed us around. "Stretch" was great at giving us the tour and goofing around. The camp is just about ready for the first round of campers.

I suspected Ani was on to me but she was actually surprised. After the tour, Stretch told us it was custom to walk a lap around the lake, engage in "deep discussion", and visit the chapel before leaving. Perfect set up. I wasn't sure what to talk about as we made our way around the lake. I made small talk with Ani about the trip last summer, scrambling to think of what I was going to say. By the time we arrived at the chapel, I was still blanking on what to say or how to ask her. Stretch was in there already waiting in the back as planned. You were already exposed for Adoration on the altar and we took a seat in the second row from the front, on the left. As we sat and prayed, I had some serious butterflies in my stomach. It was a good ten to fifteen minutes before I got the courage to speak. I mumbled something about how I asked You for permission for her as we sat after kneeling on the floor in Adoration. I then moved to one knee and pulled out the black box with the ring.

I had that ring in my back pocket all day and was worried about whether or not she could see it popping out or if I would squish it on the two and a half hour drive from Joe's. I mean the box wasn't one of those clam shell, pocket sized boxes, this thing was like a watch box in my back pocket. Literally a pain in the ass.

It was fine and beautiful but not nearly as much as she looked. She was speechless and just nodded "yes". Enter the waterworks. I even teared up. We hugged and kissed and walked to the back where Stretch was taking pictures. A couple of other missionaries clapped despite being on a silent day.

While just the beginning, I am excited to be starting this life off. It feels new. I feel confident. This is my Vocation. Figuring it out has been oppressive. A real struggle of trust but I do trust You Lord.

Random note, it was "Caturday" for the missionaries, so most of them were wearing cat shirts.

June 5, 2015—Chestnut Ridge on the Knoll by Shelter 31 and the Orchard

Back to the battle. I have been feeling fearful, anxious, and depleted lately. My work ethic and sense of self-confidence has been running low. Feeling beat up and worn down. We leave tomorrow for Life Teen's Convention in Arizona. I'm not only anxious for the flight, but I'm weary of investing the time and effort to do another commitment at St. Greg's.

I decided to get out into the woods again so I headed back to the Ridge. I started out fearful with a lot on the mind. Through the woods, along the stream, passing the orchard, I walked along on edge, stressed out. A storm was brewing overhead and twigs and sticks were rustling about. Fear had a hold on my heart. I became aware of this and started to reflect on it and began a stream of Hail Marys in decades. Still walking, I climbed a hill where the remains of an old monument sat at the top. I pressed on through the woods and entered into a clearing.

I had to burn some of the stress wearing on me so I dropped down and started doing pushups. After, I tested my strength on some fallen trees, dead lifting them to exhaustion. I tried to get one of the logs onto my shoulders for squats but failed to make it work out. So I started to run. After running back to the car I did a sequence of steam engines, mountain climbers, and pull ups. All the while, I was reflecting on my need to get disciplined: physically, mentally, spiritually, and emotionally. I don't want to live in fear or have it run my life. It's time for a game plan. Bring that flight on. Bring that career on. Bring life on.

Motivating song: "Stay" by Tenth Avenue North

June 10, 2015
Scottsdale, Arizona, CYMC

Lord, I'm here. I'm in Arizona for the Life Teen Catholic Youth Ministry Convention. I'll collect my thoughts about the whole thing later but we have a couple of minutes and I just wanted to reflect on the Mass we just had. Lord, thank you for working on my wounded heart. I just want to love and serve You with my work. I want to provide for my family and give them the most out of life.

I'm not sure where You want me. I see youth ministry laid out before me at St. Greg's and it has a lot of promise, but my heart is resistant to investing myself, to re-entering the fight there. The past three years have left me bitter and depleted. I don't want to fight for them anymore. I don't want my family to be a part of it. All that fighting has set us up for success there, but God, I have given my <u>all</u>. I'm not sure if there is more to give. If I leave, where do I go? A path I resist or a path covered in fog?

Lord, I ask that You help me at this juncture. I need to make a decision in my heart. If You want me to continue at St. Greg's, charge my heart and fill me with desire. If there is another path, reveal it and give me peace.

Actually, give me peace either way. Bless our family with the means to provide and serve You.

June 14, 2015
The Man Closet

I had a crazy set of dreams last night about our daughter, a time traveling, heroine. She had dark hair and could sing. I had the perspective of a third person observer and was able to follow her around through different ages. At some point I conversed with someone in the 19th century, telling them that I have been to 2015, of course to their wonder.

I don't recall her name but she did go to a Catholic college on the west coast. As an observer, I did witness her defy her parents so she could help others without us knowing the reasons. Lack of sleep? Prophesy? Makings for a good story? Who knows, but man I have some wild dreams. We'll see.

July 7, 2015 – Confirmation Retreat #1
St. Columban Center

Lord, I think I ate raw chicken today. Not feeling so hot.

But in other news... Thank you for the recent blessings. I had a conversation with Fr. Leon a week or so ago about youth ministry at St. Greg's. We met at the rectory at 8:30p.m. and finished at 12:30a.m. It was a long and necessary talk. Thank you for the courage to ask for a raise, to hire help, and to lead the ship. Thanks for letting me do so with tact.

The next morning, Fr. Leon called to tell me of my raise, a 1/3 more of what I was already making, and that I will lead the new hire. Thanks for the vote of confidence and answering my prayers and providing an open door to stay.

This gives me the confidence that You want me here and that I can take care of my family. You provide Lord. You answer prayers. While a small part of me wants to apply for this available position elsewhere, I am beginning to feel at home for the first time at St. Greg's, unlike the outsider I once did.

I want to also thank you for the two years with Ani. We just celebrated our Ani-versary a few days ago, which marks the longest relationship I've had with a girl, and she'll remain that way for the rest of my life, with Your blessing of course. I love her and can't wait for our big day so that we can start our family less than a year from now.

I love You Lord. I love Your daughter. Thank you.

Also, please don't let me get sick from the chicken... thanks.

August 5, 2015 – Confirmation Retreat #2
St. Columban Center

I had the opportunity to leave St. Greg's. Jim departed my home parish and I felt a pull on my heart to apply. It's my home parish after all. I've often thought about what I would do there. Ani and I are looking to live in the south towns and I would love for our family to grow in and through ministry in the place I live. There is a lot of potential there and I would love to serve again with my siblings.

I'm grateful that I was offered an interview that was held with all three priests in discretion. I didn't want anyone to know I was going for it so there wouldn't be any undue drama. The first question one of them said to me upon entering the room was, "What is it going to take to get you here?" I didn't want to assume I got the job but he put all the cards on the table rather quickly, which he promptly picked up with real questions afterwards.

The church had a split youth ministry with another parish nearby. The interview was easy to navigate but was telling of the relationship between the two pastors: two very different visions for youth ministry. I was left with more questions than answers, even with bonus time at the end. While they matched my salary, the assistant, and other resources were left in the fog.

In a conversation after the interview, the pastor confirmed my general assessment of the situation. It's kind of a mess and needs work to navigate the waters. After speaking with Ani it was clear that it wouldn't make sense to leave St. Greg's. It's finally in a good place and we're growing. We're hiring a new middle school youth minister, have a great organization, and pastor backing me up. So I called the pastors and declined the position.

I was feeling at peace until the day after I declined. I had a great deal of remorse for turning it down. Something was pulling on me. I know that I made a decision and thought I discerned it well until I got a text from Joe about thinking long term and it got me reconsidering my position. I want to have Ani as part of my ministry. I want to be present to go to Mass with her every week. I want our family to grow up in that. While my time has passed, I'm sure with reason, I'll be more conscience of these desires on my heart. I want to serve You and my family well. My eyes are open for the next opportunity. Thank you.

August, 2015
The Man Closet

I had a dream last night, more of a nightmare. It had a lot going on in it but it was the last part before I awoke that had me down. Ani died in my arms. Her last words were, "We lived a good life." It was heartbreaking and I immediately awoke. I know it's a dream but I don't spend a lot of time thinking about our mortality. Lord, she was still young. Please protect her and shield us from catastrophe. Let us live long prosperous lives in You so one day when that day comes we can say, "We lived a good life."

I trust You with our family. I love You Lord.

September 11, 2015
The Man Closet

Lord, I went to Confession last Saturday with the intent to scrub down my heart from the muck getting in the way of loving Ani fully. Every time I've gone recently, I've ignored the lustful sins that have taken a toll on me. Thank you for letting me be bold and go to the basilica with determination. Like TNT, I felt them clear out with purpose. Now I'm ready to get back to loving and building our relationship. I just finished writing my first hand written letter to her. I want to open up more to her and have us begin digging deeper in our relationship. We don't get to spend a lot of time together right now so I want to find other ways of romancing my bride to be.

I'm finishing "Rome Sweet Home" by Scott and Kim Hahn and I'm loving it. Their witness together is inspiring me in my Vocation. Scott's journey as the spiritual leader in his family is an example to me. Help me to lead my family well Lord. Help me to love Ani more fully and completely.

Songs building me up for Confession and recharging for Ani: "Iesu, Dulcis, Memoria", "Cathedrals", and "Stay" by Tenth Avenue North

Thanks Lord.

September 11, 2015
Letter to Ani

Hello my Love,

I'm writing to you today because I love you. I don't get to see you often enough for us to continually live it and show it. It is too easy to get caught up in the work life or planning process that I forget to build our relationship.

I hope that this letter is refreshing to you. In a day where communication is cheap and quick, I wanted to take the time, slow down, and hand write for you. I have been pondering our relationship and I feel as though time is flying closer to our first day of marriage without us growing closer, I offer this up to you as a remedy.

On our big day I will give you my journal to read. It is my story of finding you through God. I want to let you read the first few lines I wrote when I started with "Message to my wife":

"I love you babe.

I think about you often. I wonder who you'll be or what your name is. I've spent my life praying for you..."

As I write this and look at the year, I realize it was the year I started at St. Bernadette's and working Edge with you on the team. God is good! I'm blown away at the moment because this means God was working on us since after I wrote the first lines in my journal that same year.

So it continues and soon you'll be able to read it. Let's prepare right and with purpose.

I would like to dedicate Song of Songs for us in our engagement time. "Ah, you are beautiful, my beloved, ah, you are beautiful." Song of Songs 4:1

Adam

November 11, 2015
Praise and Worship Night at St. Greg's

It's been a while since I last wrote and time is flying by. We just hired a new youth minister, Nicole. She's been here about a month and it's already made a huge difference. While I feel fatigued in ministry and may take some time to recover my energy, it's nice to know I have relief with middle school. Thank you for the support.

I'd like to lift up Fr. Leon who is in the battle. It really does seem like the same fight I waged when I got here. Give him the strength, perseverance, and endurance to accomplish all that needs to be done. Dissolve all the walls he faces and allow him to push further than even he knows to be possible.

Lord, I'd like to pray for my relationship with Ani. It's been six months since the proposal. We're both under the stress of life. She's working three jobs and I think it's beating her up. On top of that, I don't think I'm being the man I'm capable of. I've been losing patience with her in the times she's cranky and emotional. I really need to be a better support for her.

On top of THAT, I'm running short on passion and find myself fatigued, which is making me lose focus on her and You in our relationship. I'd like to lift Ani up to You. Help her to have rest and endurance through this time. Lord, she is an amazing woman. Help her to be the best that she can be. Fill her heart with life. Allow me to be the best man I can be for her. Charge me up for my mission for her. Help us to prepare for marriage and let this be time to lay the right foundation for our family.

Lord, help us to find our home. Let us be wise yet fulfilled. Thank you Lord. We need You to be at our heart. Open our hearts to be aware of this when we fail and succeed, You alone command our hearts and relationship. Without You, we lose the heart and soul of our relationship which makes it ultimately shallow and withered.

I'm currently writing this at the Praise and Worship Night by the 4:30 group at St. Greg's. Your Spirit is moving. Thank you.

December 30, 2015
South Buffalo Apartment
4:58a.m.

> I'm laying awake at 4:30am stirring. Ani and I have had two straight nights of screwing up and on my ride of shame home I realized that we're under assault. Everyone around me is. Mom is in the process of her third try at reconstruction and has to go in for a procedure in the morning to take care of a troubled spot, a residual clash from her battle with breast cancer.

> Mom, one of the great prayer generals in my life, is and has been under attack for a long time. She's fatigued and besieged; cancer and chemo, Aunt Peggy's death, recovery, difficulties at home with Dad, not being able to build the house on their land, etc.

Our teens, especially our now defunct and rebellious "Teen Core", are in peril. They are self-destructing. Some members on the Core Team are dealing with mess, disease, and catastrophe in their life. Peers in youth ministry are facing insurmountable odds and difficulties. I sense many are at wit's end. The list goes on.

Tonight, I had a realization that we are at war, a revelation or uncovering to see it. I've been blind to it until now. Earlier this year, October, we did a series in Life Teen on spiritual warfare. At the time I felt on guard, but felt no spiritual retribution. The devil is patient, so it seems. Through my complacency, I fell. I thought we were doing well and fell asleep. Now I'm waking up with bombs and wounded warriors all around.

I'm reminded of the scene from <u>We Were Soldiers</u> where Mel Gibson's character looks at a particular messy situation all around him and calls, "Broken Arrow!" for an impressive and life saving show of air support. Lord, I'm calling for air support. "Broken Arrow!"

I'm realizing my role as commander in this war and need to start securing the perimeter, putting out the fires, tending to the wounded, and starting the counter offensive. The Vietnam imagery brings me to Fr. Capodanno. Help me to be as fearless, brave, and faithful as he was.

I think this awakening is appropriate considering the Core Training next weekend and I'm giving the Friday Night Kick off talk titled, "Battle Lines".

Let me rest tonight because tomorrow we go to battle.

Questions for you

1. What is holding you back from giving God your all? Why?
2. What needs to happen for you to surrender to Him? Why?
3. What does the "Broken Arrow" call mean to you?

Challenges:

– Consider giving God the reins to your life. It starts by telling Him that and following through by believing it every day after.

– Open up the book of Proverbs. Hit repeat. Hit repeat again. Go back often.

The Lord called me from birth, from my mother's womb he gave me my name. He made of me a sharp-edged sword and concealed me in the shadow of His arm.

ISAIAH 49: 1-6

CHAPTER FIVE

The Sword

The freshly anointed craftsman closed the doors to his new workshop after a long day. He tucked his sheathed, prized project under his arm and headed down the cobbled street. He made his way across town to see his master. After a friendly greeting, the craftsman unsheathed and presented the master with his greatest and most beautiful weapon, "I want to thank you for teaching me how to master this craft. This is my greatest work and I want to give it to you."

The master slowly reached out and accepted the gift, proud of his pupil's work. While cautiously inspecting the crafted weapon in his rough hands, he thought about what each skill was applied to this fine work. After a few moments he replied, "Your greatest work is always still ahead."

◆

The long and hard process of formation is completed when the blacksmith's vision has come to fruition—the finished product is ready to do what it was designed for.

What are you made for in this life? What gifts and talents do you have? What weaknesses do you have? What is He asking you to do?

I used to think that purpose came with clarity, and I didn't proceed or take action until I had that. Your purpose is known, but it may not be known by you, yet. The analogy of iron only goes so far—unlike the iron, we have free will. Our Blacksmith gives us our hopes and dreams and when rightly ordered in Him, there is peace in those decisions. Trust where He's planted you and lean into that. We are always being formed and reformed in this life.

Maybe you are young, fresh, and eager to get at it. Maybe you've been in the battle and need repair. Trust and act.

◆

December 31, 2015
Nativity Chapel
7:10p.m.

> Lord, today marks the end of maybe the best year of my life, even through the battle. I finished college, proposed marriage to my future wife, and today signed for our first house. "My soul proclaims the greatness of the Lord."
>
> Thank you for the abundance of blessings in my life. This house is a cut above everything else we were looking at. Thank you for all the circumstances that led us here. I pray for our family. Keep us healthy and safe in the New Year. I pray that our lives serve You well. Happy New Year Lord. 2015 has been rocky but ultimately great.

January 19, 2016
Blasdell Apartment
11:52 p.m.

> I feel ashamed. Earlier today I had to admit that I am struggling with cold feet. I don't know why I am losing sight of my love. On top of that, I am feeling depleted at work. An anger and friction is building on my heart and I feel like I am taking it out on Nicole.

> Wounded warrior: I feel like I have been struck and need a medic. Not sure how or where it came from but I know this isn't going to be a quick recharge. I need help. Medic!

February 24, 2016
Canisius College Chapel
8:01 p.m.

> Lord, I give You these struggles. I find comfort in knowing that I can trust You with my healing. Open up my heart for it. Open up my eyes to see it. Whatever it takes to stay my heart.

> Listening to "Stay" by 10th Avenue North

> Just met with Fr. Marty for spiritual direction.

> As St. John Neumann put it, there are periods of ups known as, "consolation"; when you are spiritually well, take care not to get drunk on the high. When the spirit is withdrawn, you get to the point of "desolation". Don't despair in desolation and follow the saints in this. St. Teresa of Calcutta, St. Pio, St. Peter, St. Therese of Lisieux, pray for us.

THE SWORD

March 27, 2016 (Easter)
Blasdell Apartment
9:26 a.m.

Happy Easter Lord! Alleluia!

It's a beautiful day outside. I'm just laying in bed pondering life. It is quiet with the exception of passing cars. There is less than one week until I am in the new house. Thank you for this blessing. This will probably be the last quiet Easter and certainly the last one waking up by myself. I'm excited for the new life that is developing: marriage, homeownership, fire to move in my career, the desire to build new relationships and fix old ones. I feel like I am coming out of this Lent like I have been traveling in a desert: thirsty, burned, and tired. But now, on to fertile land.

Thank you for making me a better man. Keep it up! Thank you for dying for us and saving us from death. Amen.

April 9, 2016
New House
5:20 pm

And... I'm in the new house. It's a mixed bag of emotions. I love it here. I've had a few fires in the stove, got most of the unpacking done, even had a couple of friends over last night. The move was smooth and went by quickly with all of the help we had. With the exception of Jeremy tearing off the wallpaper strip in the kitchen, the house is in good order.

Enter Ani. She's been fried working all year on overdrive with her three jobs. During the move, it was apparent that she wasn't in a good mood and just got worse post move. No excitement or enthusiasm. Pouty. During this time of celebration she's down and out. She calls it a "dark place".

I try to talk to her about it and she doesn't want to. I tried cheering her up and I get snarky comments. I even tried giving her space, which erupted into a fight over text. It's really hurting us and I'm starting to react negatively. I've noticed I've been more distant, snippy, and stressed (if that's possible).

I'm so worried our relationship is so wounded that I've pondered postponing the wedding. We had a great talk earlier in the week where I expressed my concerns. I even mentioned that she should see a doctor. Ani says it's hormones with all the big changes just multiplying it. I think it is something more. What I do know is we haven't seen joy in a while. We see each other quickly once or twice a week with a dedicated date night every other Monday. I don't want to start out marriage out like this. I'm not willing to walk up to the altar feeling this way.

Fortunately, Ani is almost done with her semester. I hope the end of her burden provides us the time to heal and recover.

Lord, I'd like to pray for Ani to get out of the hole she is in. Help her to know that she is worthy of love and is beautiful. Help her to use this experience to grow as a woman and let her be the best that she can be and never revisit this again.

Lord, help me to be loving, understanding, supportive, and patient… because… I'm running low.

In unrelated news, help me to find a job I can say "yes" to. Bless my footsteps forward as I cross the stream.

First post in the new house, wish it was happier.

April 9, 2016
New House
9:48p.m.

Actually, driving around today cleared my mind. If I'm going to be the man I'm made to be, the man made to love, the man who doesn't run, then I need to be strong for Ani. Hard times will come. I was made to respond better than this.

April 15, 2016
Spring Retreat: "Glorify", Camp Kenan
10:30p.m.

Lord, I am on another Spring Retreat. I just handed out Life Teen journals to the teens. They are writing down their conversation with You.

I'm not sure where to go with this; they are actually writing! Woohoo!

While I was walking around outside under the stars while they were in Small Group, I kept thinking about what's next for me. I'm back to the end-of-year burnout and feeling ready to move on. Guide my footsteps and help me move.

April 16, 2016
Spring Retreat: "Glorify", Camp Kenan
10a.m.

It's Saturday morning on retreat. I'm really not feeling this one. Trying to, Lord, but it just feels deflated. But I will keep trying. Whatever this needs to be Lord, I give it to You.

We started off the session with the "Garden Game" (soil, seed, and water poured on contestants should they get an answer wrong. Classic.). Amy talked about Mary Magdalene afterwards and how she did not understand who You were after the Resurrection. She called You "teacher" without the full understanding of what You've accomplished. Help me to understand better too.

April 16, 2016
Spring Retreat: "Glorify", Camp Kenan
8pm

Morgan is giving a talk about Lazarus. Her question for us is this: "When was a time that we wanted a prayer answered and it wasn't answered as we wanted?" Like Mary and Martha's desire for Jesus to be there at the right time to heal their brother. Hmmm.

THE SWORD

April 18, 2016
Home
12:28 a.m.

Lord, Thank you for taking this retreat to a better place. It turned out better than I thought. Even up to departure back home, I wasn't spiritually or emotionally moved. It just felt like work, like my gut wasn't in it to win it.

Something changed on the ride back home with Ross and Chris. I had the old Newsboys album, "Go" on and the guys were taking notes on song titles. We reminisced over Kingdom Bound last year where we saw For King and Country. They requested a song off the "Run Wild" album, so I put it on. Ross then said out of the blue, "Hey Adam, has anyone ever told you that you're the greatest guy ever?"

It was nice to hear but I just shrugged it off with a "no, not lately Ross", thinking he was just messing around.

Chris backed him up saying, "Yea Adam, I agree with Ross."

It brought a smile to my face but what hit me in the gut was the follow up from Ross, "No, I'm serious Adam; I feel like I am closer to God because of you." Chris agreed.

Wow. I'm not sure I have ever heard that before. Almost four years of being a youth minister and never heard that. I've heard that I'm doing good work or cool things but never actually doing the one thing I'm here to do and that's leading teens closer to You. Certainly not from a kid.

Just as I started thinking about that, the song that I usually skip on the album comes on, "Run Wild". I've listened to the song a ton of times before but just moved on. I didn't even think about the song when it came on, as my mind was still with what the guys said. Then I hear, "Adam, are you a lion who lost his roar?"

Gut shot.

Assuming he was talking about the song, I didn't know how to answer. I don't even remember how I did. I don't even remember that line in the song. I had to rehear it and after the kids were dropped off, I went back to it. Sure enough, "You're a lion full of power who forgot how to roar."

That hit me sideways.

That line is so loaded. I feel that. I think I'm living that. I've loved watching lions and other big cats; my dad use to call me "Tiger" as a kid. There is something spectacular about a full-grown lion that stands apart from all of the others: king of the jungle, man-eater, full of power, majesty. The lion was used by England in the coat of arms in the Middle Ages; C.S. Louis used the lion to represent the Almighty; African tribes would use lion-hunting as a rite of passage into manhood.

There are faster cats like cheetahs, smarter animals like chimps, stronger like bulls or oxen, bigger like elephants, tougher like rhinos, but a lion? That's fearsome.

THE SWORD

Last year, Ani and I went to the zoo. Aside from the fun of spending time with Ani, it was a somewhat disappointing visit. I remember feeling pity over the caged animals. They looked depressed. The wild long gone. I specifically remember the tiger pacing back and forth, lost. Just staring as it wondered. That was a tiger who had forgotten how to roar.

So if I am a lion who has lost his roar, how do I get it back?

Back in the woods, this is one to chew on. Lord, help me to recharge my heart through the end-of-year burnout. Let me roar and be wild at heart again. Let me love strong and live free like the lion on the Serengeti.

April 28, 2016
Home on Dirkson (still working on a good name for the place. Casa de Jarosz?)
8:16p.m.

Lord, I feel Your healing taking place between Ani and I. It's towards the end of the school year for her, last week in fact. We're doing a lot better. Thank you for that but especially for teaching me to respond better during tenuous times. Help me to support her even in the most difficult times. I love her and want to be the best I can be for her.

I'm sitting at the desk for the first time with my computer and a copy of <u>The Fellowship of the Ring</u>: the greatest story I have ever read. I just started typing out my journal. I offer this to You. I feel like the experiences given to me need to be shared. I pray someone makes use of this so they may not feel alone in their struggle or even that it may benefit a community by supporting their youth minister. I offer this for Your glory and not my own. I ask for the intercession of Blessed Pier Giorgio Frassati so my efforts reach the heights. I want to defeat the temptation of mediocrity and complacency.

In Your name, I pray.

May 31, 2016
3:37 a.m.

Today marked a significant milestone for Ani and I. It was three years since our first date, one year since we got engaged, two months since we closed on the house, and a little over a month until we are married. It was a beautiful day out. We bought our first mattress and the paint for the kitchen. Ani's family had a nice party for Memorial Day and I'm glad I got to spend time with them.

It's crazy how turbulent this year has been: the ups and the downs, the growing pains and joys. Even looking further out to when I first started writing in this book or since I graduated high school. Thank you for this road and for teaching me how to love, for sending me Ani, teaching me how to love her better, and lastly, not making me a priest.

I go to bed tonight in peace with my mind certain of love for Ani as I recall her wrapped up with me watching the movie tonight but also when we were at Fr. Sam's first

THE SWORD

Mass at St. Greg's. I felt a genuine joy for him and the brotherhood. I no longer fear the priesthood like I once did. Knowing my Vocation now has settled into a peace only You can give on my heart.

Priests are very special and I ask that You continue to lift them up. Of course, Lord, if it is Your will, and theirs, I would be proud if You used one of our future sons for the priesthood, perhaps the first American pope? You heard it here first.

June 26, 2016
Casa de Jarosz
12:19p.m.

We are a week away from being married and it's been a busy day. Got frustrated with the work on the master bedroom and the terrible wallpaper, booked our Disney and Universal tickets, changed hotels, wrote out a checklist, did laundry, mowed the lawn, and went to Home Depot twice and Lowes once.

As busy as it is, I took notice of two things today. While driving home I saw the sunset and recalled the times I would wrestle with You over finding my wife at Woodlawn. It's been a while since then and I just wanted to thank You for bringing me to the sunset of singlehood. I'll have more to share on that later. The second thing was witnessing two love birds (literal birds, robins) doing the dance. The male was chasing the female around the street in front of me while I sat on the porch: flying, hopping, chirping; love is in the air and it's contagious. Let's get this started!

July 2, 2016
Casa de Jarosz, Back Porch
7 a.m.

It's here. Today is our wedding day. I'm up early sitting outside. It's a beautiful day. The sun is golden, sky blue, birds chirping. Perfect start.

This has been one heck of a journey. I have had to grow so much to get here. Thank you for bringing me through to this day, every step and lesson learned (over and over again in some cases). Thank you for the opportunity to catalog this road in this journal. Most of all, thank you for Ani, my soon to be wife. She is an incredible woman and I couldn't have picked a better person to spend the rest of my life and build a family with. Thank you for keeping me in it when I was stupid and immature and could have walked away.

Ani, my bride, my love, I'm so ready for you. After reading this, I hope that you see how God had to craft me for you. I had to say "yes" to Him before I could say "yes" to you and before you could say "yes" to me. Today we both say "I do". I hope and will strive to be the best man I can be for you. It is my pledge to always love you and continue to grow for you and our family. I want to be the best that I can be spiritually, emotionally, physically, and mentally for you. I love you with all that I am and will be. I now give my life to you so we can both give to God.

Let's get this party started!

July 12, 2016
Parc Solei Resort, Orlando

We're on our last day of the honeymoon in Orlando. It's been awesome. Our stay in Miami at the Ritz-Carlton was very nice. One can say... ritzy. Our room overlooked the ocean, service was impeccable, and the breakfast was delicious (and included thankfully, after looking at the bill). Top-tier food on the buffet; smoked salmon, prosciutto, omelet station, berries, champagne, just goes on and on. Big iguanas were all over the place running after fallen food, sometimes jumping on tables. Of course we would choose the outdoor seating and watch the pool and ocean. Seriously, like a movie.

We spent a day at the Miami Zoo and loved checking it all out. The heat was a little much but we survived. Met up with Nhan and his wife over more good food at a fantastic fusion restaurant. All you can eat steak, seafood, and sushi. We chose to leave Miami early to go to Key West, long drive but worth it. Margaritas at Margaritaville, kayaking out to an island, and pulling off Route 1 for a dip in the wild, blue water.

We ended our trip in Orlando with a stay in Disney and a visit to Universal. You can't go wrong there and we loved our time together. What a great start to a wonderful life.

July 19, 2016
Casa de Jarosz
2:31 a.m.

We've been following Ani's cycle since before we were married. We were expecting her to have her period before we left Orlando annnnd it never came. Even before that, mere days after our wedding night, she mentioned how she was feeling different. I suspected, a baby then. I just had a feeling.

We met a darling woman who checked us in at the Ritz named Marisol. Loved the name and she took great care of us. As a running joke over the honeymoon, I'd rub Ani's stomach and talk to it as if the baby was starting up, naming it Marisol. Adorbs.

We left Miami early after going to the mall and stopping at the Disney store. Seeing all of the baby princess stuff and imagining our little girl in Disney stuff was just too much. One of the most exciting and moving things I've ever felt, was thinking about how we would be able to create life. First thoughts of parenting were overwhelming. So we packed up early and went to Disney dreaming of a baby.

THE SWORD

As time passed, it became more apparent that she was late for a reason. We almost bought a pregnancy test in Key West but we resisted.

The day after we came home Ani was getting ready upstairs, and after a while, I went up to check on her. She was crying and apologizing. I saw the pregnancy test on the shelf and I knew. She wanted to surprise me but the test was negative. After I comforted her, we both agreed that it was OK and it just means not right now.

However, I wasn't convinced of the result.

Listening to how Ani's body was behaving and her period not showing up screamed something was up.

Today after dinner, Ani said she had a surprise. After looking up information about the pregnancy tester she thinks she misinterpreted it. She thinks we will be having a baby!! Marisol!

Let me backtrack a second...

We had the honor of taking Bishop Michael and Fr. Justus, both from Tanzania, out to dinner on Saturday. Fr. Leon and the other priests were unable to be free to entertain our visitors at St. Greg's for one of the evenings of their stay. They asked the staff if anyone would be willing to take them out for dinner, and after asking Ani, I agreed to it.

So we went out for a fun evening with our guests to 800 Maple. Good food and conversation. I loved hearing about the Church in Africa and what life was like in their communities. The bishop blessed us at the beginning and at the end told us to watch for the Gospel during Mass the next day.

The readings were highly relevant. 1st reading—Genesis 18:1-10a. Abraham gave warm hospitality to traveling strangers. After a feast they said to him, "Where is your wife?" Abraham replied, "There in the tent."

One said, "I will surely return to you about the same time next year and Sarah will have a son." Today, the following day, Ani reveals that she may be pregnant after all!

The Gospel reading: Luke 10: 38-42. Martha and Mary. The table needed to be cleaned up after dinner and the dishes needed to be done.

Ani was anxious to go through our wedding pictures tonight and started the dishes. I felt like we should pray about the good news of the baby but she wanted to wait until after we were all cleaned up. Making the connection to the Gospel reading and Martha and Mary, I suggested we not be Martha. We then ran to the couch and gave thanks.

Thank you Lord for my wife and new baby.

Praise You.

Now is baby, a girl, Marisol, or a boy... is the bishop on point with the reading in Genesis?

THE SWORD

August 6, 2016
Casa de Jarosz
10:39 a.m.

I'm a couple of days in from returning from World Youth Day, Krakow. Aside from catching up on sleep and spending time with Ani I have been reflecting on my time overseas. Leading up to the trip, my mind has been preoccupied with getting married. I also had some anxiety over the security of the event. With an uptick in terror attacks in Europe, I, among others, couldn't help but think of the opportunity such a gathering of 2 million Christians would offer enemies looking to make a mark. Security was tight but a dedicated terrorist could make a mess.

A priest we were traveling with mentioned the apprehension of a would-be-assailant in Germany, whose intention was to target World Youth Day. On July 26, 2016, Fr. Jacques Hamel was martyred in Normandy, France by Muslim men who slit his throat while he was saying Mass. His last words were "Be gone Satan!" A tribute for this man at the catechesis arena was a stark reminder of the real danger that exists.

I was blindsided by the profound effect World Youth Day had on me spiritually and emotionally. I was apprehensive about this trip and didn't expect anything from it. Even from the early days of planning, I remember telling Ani that I probably wasn't going. It was a long-running joke that I sadly recognized wasn't going to be a reality.

The trip wasn't easy either. The group dynamics of our troupe proved to be complex and difficult to navigate. If I was a better leader and prepared for this, perhaps I could have done better, but as it was, those I was responsible for became the least favorite part of the pilgrimage. It became a lesson in mercy. I asked Ani early in my trip to pray for my patience. There were many times I should have lost my cool but didn't, thank God.

With the baby on the way, I found myself really emotional at the thought of fatherhood. I choked up many times and found tears during Adoration in the arena. There was so much imagery that I found applying to my new Vocation. To name just a few: While we waited for a speaker to reflect on the Auschwitz experience, a video played on the stages of development of a baby and struck at home for me. One of the dads traveling with us gave an awesome example of the selfless love of a father to his discouraging daughters. Or even the playing of "Good Good Father" in Adoration immediately after my prayer for fatherhood.

I also gained a new appreciation for my Polish heritage on this trip. I grew up often ashamed of being Polish. The great-grandparents fled Poland because of conscription by the Russians. They came here with nothing to be American and left the Old World behind. They didn't pass on the language because there was no need to look back. The only thing left over to me of that heritage was kielbasa, Dyngus Day, and my last name, which has been Americanized.

I saw through history, Poland get run over time and time again, often being occupied and kicked around. I saw no heroism in these people. I always had an image of serfs tending to middle-age farms, not unlike the <u>Monty Python and the Holy Grail</u> scene where the king stumbles upon the old, peasant woman, I mean man. A "Second World country" if there was such a thing.

On top of that, Poles always seemed to be the butt of jokes growing up. I saw "Pollock" as a curse word. "How many Pollock's does it take…" suggested the Poles are intellectually backwards.

What I learned from being there, however, helped me overcome a lifetime of misunderstanding and ignorance. Between my real experiences and the book "City of Saints", my false perception became pride. Poland has a rich history of valor, culture, faith, architecture, art, and more. I couldn't have been more wrong.

I left my journal behind for Ani to read and jotted some entries in the Pilgrim Journal. I'm going to copy them here.

---From Monday July 25, 2016

Auschwitz I&II Birkneau, Rained-out Lunch on the Bus, Visit to Kalwaria, Zebrydowska (JPII's Site), Dinner.

Auschwitz was a solemn experience. To witness the sight and the site where so much death occurred brought out a varying degree of anger and sorrow. Stepping through the front gates, in such a large crowd, gave me goose bumps and a chill. I imagined myself in the place of those victims in our crowd of many pilgrims being herded in by military security. It was an eerie feeling as we shuffled, closely packed, through the entrance of the original gates. Granted, we walked in on our freewill, as opposed to the prisoners shipped in on cattle car. We at least were able to leave.

It's hard to put into words the feelings about walking in the footsteps of a million people who met terrible deaths here. Seeing the railcars used to transport people like cattle, rattled my nerves. This isn't a reconstruction or replica; this is the real thing. We saw the crematoria and gas chambers that sealed the fate of a million souls, people who looked like any one of the pilgrims now if you were to swap clothes. My feet walked the same steps that many would have as their last. The well-preserved site gave my eyes the same sight they would have had minus the evil engine that drove the destruction.

One of the most challenging sites to see was the pond that the ashes from the crematoria were dumped into. It's a pond of a million souls. Better thought, the hope that all of those souls are in Heaven.

This experience really makes me think that all life has value and should be defended. So far, nothing has cemented my support of life more than this. When you read about the rise of Nazism and Hitler, it's easy to draw correlations to today. It's not some extinguished mentality that belongs to some other age. As shown with abortion, we are just as susceptible to mass graves and lies as the German people were. Same tactics: identity politics, dehumanization, and a removal of faith, logic, and reason follow us as a shadow. We must always fight for life and the dignity of the human person and against oppression.

Upon reading <u>Defying Hitler</u> a year ago, a book I won't soon forget, I learned totalitarianism and terror doesn't just fit nicely as a 20th century problem but as an ever-present threat to civilization that needs to be checked and suppressed. Like a man-eating tiger, it will consume if let out.

---From Wednesday July 27, 2016

At Adoration tonight, I prayed that I would be a good husband and father. I became emotional with the Spirit and tears flowed from my eyes. Just after I finished my prayer, "Good Good Father" was played by Matt Maher. The words felt like an answer from God. "You're a good, good father. It's who you are. It's who you are. It's who you are. It's who I am. It's who I am. It's who I am." Thank you Lord for being a good Father for me and crafting me into a good father as well.

---From Thursday July 28, 2016

Catechesis was with Cardinal Luis Antonio Tagle from the Philippines. It's a showing of pride to do everything yourself. Resist the mentality of doing it "my way" or "I am self- made". If you don't face these wounds you will be harsh on others. Christ says that if you are a lost sheep, "you are mine and your wounds can never diminish your worth to me. I will carry you if you cannot walk." Don't be a lost sheep. Accept help.

---From Friday July 29, 2016

Went to John Paul II's church and Divine Mercy Chapel. Saw JPII's vestments that he was shot in and had my rosary touch the glass. Also went to St. Faustina's convent and saw the window to the room she died in, the original Divine Mercy image, and her reliquary in the chapel. During our "mandatory fun time" I saw the Kracovian Archeological Museum and the Dominican Monastery that hosts Blessed Pier Giorgio Frassati relics. I prayed for Frassati's intercession for Pat's special intentions.

I have been feeling frustrated as a leader on this trip. A particular family has been a thorn in my side. While Jim, the father, has been great, there has been an uneasy tension with the family. Beverly, the mother, is to be had in small doses. Yesterday, we left the opening ceremony for World Youth Day with Pope Francis and took the group back up the way Josh and I went on Tuesday after getting split up in the crowd. Instead of walking as a group, Bev and her daughter Sam walked ahead taking Brian with them. Even after I addressed the group about the issue, they don't understand that we need to move as fast as our slowest member. Josh is consistently the slowest member, which leaves me to tend to him, otherwise the others would just leave him behind.

So Sam and Bev used an app that took a route different from my own. Because they ran ahead and I was stuck with bringing up the rear with Josh, I wasn't in the lead of directions. They were also running ahead, out of reach. So either I let them guide us as a group or I let them go their own way and we meet them back at the hotel. Decided we'd stick it out and let them take us back using their app. It took us off the known path, however, and down back alleys and a trail (I found out later that trail passed by the quarry JPII worked in when he was younger, which was cool). It was not just an easy stroll in the park but became a tedious trek through mud, thorn bushes, and brush. I'm all about a good adventure but going through unknown neighborhoods with those I'm responsible for, kept me edgy. Josh hasn't been in a good condition for doing rugged walking and really struggled. Seeing how Josh struggled through and being required to keep him occupied, I tried to keep my cool, but felt my patience burn away. There wasn't much care for Josh from the others, who were just looking to ditch him.

He hasn't exactly been doing himself any favors either. Often awkwardly pouty and emotional, and at times, off-putting and just being younger than the others, he had a hard time fitting in. I get it. I can see how he has worn on the others over the trip despite my encouragement to keep letting him in. I'm usually stuck trying to build him up and play Mr. Icebreaker and it's worn me out. I don't mean to gripe but I am worn out from the group dynamic. I wish I was a better leader to sort this out but my tool belt is exhausted. I don't "yearn" often, but man, I yearn to be home with Ani and baby (who is three weeks from conception).

Well this is World Youth Day and the theme and jubilee year is all about "Mercy". Plus, I just saw St. Faustina, St. John Paul II, and the Divine Mercy Image and chapel. There is no better place than right here right now to show mercy. This is Pilgrimage...

---Sunday July 31, 2016

My experience for the main event was from the hotel with Josh and some others from the Buffalo contingent who stayed behind. We watched the final Mass with Pope Francis over Chris's laptop. Josh's knee prevented him from going and making the trip to Campus Misericordia, a long haul on foot. It was bittersweet. I wanted to be out there but I didn't want him to be left alone at the hotel. The journey proved difficult for those who went, however. Heat, bugs, and exhaustion combined with torrential rain put the misery in Misericordia for many. Some couldn't handle it and came back early before even getting started.

Here are some paraphrased notes from the Pope's homily: "The Church is made up of two lungs: the East and the West", quoting St. John Paul II after the readings in Paleoslavic. "At times we aim lower rather than higher [...] Jesus is always cheering us on, our biggest fan, even when we turn ourselves in. Holding onto sadness is a virus and God wants to see us in joy. Every morning wake up and pray, 'Lord thank you for loving me." He continues, "Bring all of your thoughts to confession, even your weakness. May we remember the God who wants us here."

Sunday July 31, 2016 (after the Final Mass and waiting for everyone to return)
Divine Mercy Chapel, Krakow, Poland
1:20p.m.

I'm sitting in the chapel with St. Faustina and the Divine Mercy Image. I came here by myself to reflect and pray; some in the group who don't have an appreciation of this journey frustrates me right now. On mind right now is the mom and girls who came back early last night on a taxi after leaving their dad on the field. They left this morning to go to the mall instead of watching the final Mass. Oh, also another teen I came across, who stayed behind because he was "exhausted" and had to work eight hours when he arrived back home, so might as well rest now. It's a long walk after all. Anyways...

I'm not sure if I'm being judgmental, or just observing, or both. Show me patience and let me give mercy. My heart goes out to Jim who, as the spiritual leader of his family, sought to expose his daughters and wife to an amazing experience. He has the heart of a pilgrim here.

While he is journeying back from the overnight outdoors with the pope and two million of his closest friends in a hot and buggy field, his family is romping around in the mall after abandoning him out there. I feel symbolism in this.

The image of a father giving his all for his family only to have them reject him is potent. I wonder of the frustration, anger, and rejection he must feel. However, Jim has been patient and loving for them, at least externally. I am reminded of how You give abundantly yet some reject You.

This also reminds me of what we are up against in culture. A rejection of You for comfort and material things. Pope Francis spoke about this in his homily. He spoke to us about rejecting comfort just because it is easy and picking up our cross and faith in Jesus, which is increasingly difficult in today's climate.

Despite dragging my feet to get to Poland, I have been eager to push hard during the pilgrimage and encouraged the others not to view this as a vacation. I don't think I have appreciated how much my faith has grown over time. I forget that I'm leading them down a path where I am expecting them to be at my point in the faith journey. When I see fellow pilgrims, especially the ones in our group griping, I realize we have a long way to go to prepare their hearts for the road.

Thank you for building me up to handle this but I ask that You now help me to pass that on to my family, then to others, in a way You would be proud of. Help me to be a "Good Good Father" like You, for my family. Shield us and give us resistance through exposure, "We are in the world but not of it", for our family today and for future generations, a resistance to the secularization that has claimed many of our millennial generation.

Convert the family's girls' hearts. Let the seeds of mercy on this trip bloom in their family.

I love You Lord and despite my cold heart leading up to the trip, You have abundantly warmed and watered it. Make me lion-hearted so I can go home for You and my family. Bless my direction and next steps. Give us safe and smooth travels back home. Give this lion the hunger to still defeat lust and replace it with love. Sts. Faustina, John Paul II, and Bl. Pier Giorgio Frassati, pray for us.

August 6, 2016
Casa de Jarosz
10:39a.m.

I couldn't have asked for better timing to end an era and start a new one with the close of this journal. I pray that the witness of faith, Vocation, and ministry serve You well Lord. Thank you for the experiences that make me who I am and for the people You put in my life, especially my wife and family. I lift up the next chapter of my life to You Lord.

I think a fitting end for this is in the spirit of Divine Mercy, "Jezu Ufain Tobie": "Jesus I trust in You."

This marked the end of my first journal. Volume I.

Questions for you:

1. When was the last time you felt mercy? Refresh yourself on the story. What happened? How did it feel?

2. When was the last time you showed mercy? What were the circumstances?

3. How do you think God is preparing you to be the blade? What do you see Him doing for you now in preparation?

Challenges:

- Find a place of solitude outdoors. Hike, bike, or swim with God. Talk to Him through it. Write it down. Grow this part in your life.

- Invitation: Offer up your life to Christ right now. Redo it if you've been away for a while. Allow Him into your successes, failings, joys and fears.

- Make a commitment right now to build or rebuild spiritual discipline in your life—little by little or radical change. Take ownership of this part of your life—go to Mass, find or build a community, pray daily, seek adventure and center the Lord in it, show love and gratitude in your comings and goings. Build. Rebuild.

The Glory of God is a man fully alive, but the life of a man is the vision of God."

ST. BERNARD OF CLAIRVAUX

Epilogue

As I looked back on reading my own journal, I saw how God was building me—further prayer has led me to seeing myself as an instrument and with God as the Blacksmith, every pounding I received was a blessing. Crafting me into a better man, husband, father, and leader. By no means has my journal been a record of every day or every event, but it has certainly captured moments that helped me see His work.

This book is an invitation to keep your own story through the years. Track God's movements in your life. See how He uses every moment and stretch of consolation and desolation to build you as a heavenly weapon. Every hard moment and every joy. It doesn't have to be everyday. Maybe it's tracking the long movements of life and seeing the themes of growth.

This is my journey, it is no more important than yours. As St. Francis of Assisi told his followers on his deathbed, "I have done what is mine; may Christ teach you what is yours!" Go and live. Be formed. Be a witness to it, authentically beyond the thin veil of what the world offers. Know the Father. Know Jesus. Know the Holy Spirit. Believe the call for your heart to Heaven. This life is only so long, but there is more on the other side that we can grow numb to while traversing from one end to the other of the years on our gravestone. Awaken or reawaken to the holy. It doesn't just change your life here it builds it for the next. If you don't know where to begin, you can start by offering your heart to Jesus right now.

From there, I would suggest talking to a priest. I know, there will be those of you who roll your eyes at the Church—it's easy to do today as it's wrapped in the tentacles of the Enemy. But. The gates of Hell will not prevail in sinking the ship (Matt 16: 18). The Sacraments are God's gift to us to continue our journey in faith with His presence. There is a depth in this Tradition that has no end to it. Pop the hood on the Catholic perspective, you'll find that Bishop Fulton Sheen's words ring true:

> *There are not over a hundred people in the United States who hate the Catholic Church. There are millions, however, who hate what they wrongly believe to be the Catholic Church — which is, of course, quite a different thing. These millions can hardly be blamed for hating Catholics because Catholics "adore statues"; because they "put the Blessed Mother on the same level with God"; because they say "indulgence is a permission to commit sin"; because the Pope "is a Fascist"; because the "Church is the defender of Capitalism." If the Church taught or believed any one of these things it should be hated, but the fact is that the Church does not believe nor teach any one of them. It follows then that the hatred of the millions is directed against error and not against truth. As a matter of fact, if we Catholics believed all of the untruths and lies which were said against the Church, we probably would hate the Church a thousand times more than they*

do. If I were not a Catholic, and were looking for the true Church in the world today, I would look for the one Church which did not get along well with the world; in other words, I would look for the Church which the world hates... Look for the Church that is hated by the world, as Christ was hated by the world. Look for the Church which is accused of being behind the times, as Our Lord was accused of being ignorant and never having learned. Look for the Church which men sneer at as socially inferior, as they sneered at Our Lord because He came from Nazareth. Look for the Church which is accused of having a devil, as Our Lord was accused of being possessed by Beelzebub, the Prince of Devils. Look for the Church which, in seasons of bigotry, men say must be destroyed in the name of God as men crucified Christ and thought they had done a service to God. Look for the Church which the world rejects because it claims it is infallible, as Pilate rejected Christ because He called Himself the Truth. Look for the Church which is rejected by the world as Our Lord was rejected by men... If then, the hatred of the Church is founded on erroneous beliefs, it follows that basic need of the day is instruction. Love depends on knowledge for we cannot aspire nor desire the unknown. Our great country is filled with what might be called marginal Christians, i.e., those who live on the fringe of religion and who are descendants of Christian living parents, but who now are Christians only in name. They retain a few of its ideals out of indolence and force of habit; they knew the glorious history of Christianity only through certain emasculated forms of it, which have married the spirit of the age and are now dying with it. Of Catholicism and its sacraments, its pardon, its grace, its certitude and its peace, they know nothing except a few inherited prejudices. And yet they are good people who want to do the right thing, but who have no definite philosophy concerning it. They educate their children without religion, and yet they resent the compromising morals of their children. They would be angry if you told them they were not Christian, and yet they do not believe that Christ is God. They resent being called pagans and yet they never take a practical cognizance of the existence of God. There is only one thing of which they are certain and that is that things are not right as they are. It is just that single certitude which makes them what might be called the great "potentials," for they are ready to be pulled in either of two directions. Within a short time they must take sides; they must either gather with Christ or they must scatter; they must either be with Him or against Him; they must either be on the cross as other Christs, or under it as other executioners. Which way will these marginal Christians tend?... Only this much is certain. Being human and having hearts they want more than class struggle and economics; they want Life, they want Truth, and they want Love. In a word, they want Christ. It is to these millions who believe wrong things about the Church and to these marginal Christians, that this little book is sent. It is not to prove that they are "wrong"; it is not to prove that we are "right"; it is merely to present the truth in order that the truth may conquer through the grace of God."

EPILOGUE

Since the end of this journal, I pick up where I leave it here with Volume II. I continue to track God's work and document the lessons and moments in my life that act as a lesson to my family tree and a witness to God's work. I'll have more to say about this another time. As I feel the end of one age here, an age of discernment and honing, it starts a greater journey—raising our family. The blessings will continue to grow and the challenges will become more difficult as life advances. I pray that I'm well equipped to rise to the occasion. There will be ups and downs, but I know that God is with me. As a later volume will reveal, I know I'm made by Great Love and for hard things. When I fail, I know God is with me. When I succeed, I know God is with me. I pray that I may lead my family well and most importantly that we flourish in faith, "as for me and my household, we will serve the Lord," Joshua 24:15.

Following God requires our everything. He wants us to come to Him. If He is who He says He is, then everything from creation to the way we live, is a response to that invitation. If you have been sleeping your way through belief or have never believed, I pray that you open your heart to the most challenging and rewarding adventure you'll ever know.

As Pope Benedict XVI said, "You were not made for comfort, you were made for greatness." Give this life your all and your all to God and you will see miracles unfold before your eyes.

Go out there. Dream. Do. Be righteous. I'll see you in the further refined, Volume II.

–Adam

Dream. Do. Be. Righteous.

ADAM JAROSZ, FOUNDER

RIGHTEOUS CO.

The journey continues with Righteous Co.

Follow along with us at **righteousco.com**

@righteousco  @righteousco

To Marisol Jarosz, our first

August 9, 2016

Rest in Peace, Baby

www.ingramcontent.com/pod-product-compliance
Lightning Source LLC
Chambersburg PA
CBHW050815090426
42736CB00021B/3458